1149130

W9-ACE-035

THEO | THE OTHER VAN GOGH

THEO | THE OTHER VAN GOGH

MARIE-ANGÉLIQUE OZANNE & FRÉDÉRIQUE DE JODE

TRANSLATED BY ALEXANDRA BONFANTE-WARREN

A MARK MAGOWAN BOOK

THE VENDOME PRESS

First published in the United States of America by
Magowan Publishing LLC and The Vendome Press
1334 York Avenue
New York, NY 10021

ISBN: 0-86565-236-8

Library of Congress Cataloging-in-Publication Data

Ozanne, Marie Angélique.
  [Autre Van Gogh: English]
  Theo : the other Van Gogh / Marie Angélique & Frédérique de
Jode ; translated by Alexandra Bonfante-Warren.
      p. cm.
      "A Mark Magowan book."
      Includes bibliographical references and index.
      ISBN: 086565-236-8 (alk. paper)
      1. Gogh, Theo van, 1857-1891. 2. Art dealers--Netherlands--
Biography. I. Jode, Frédérique de. II. Title.

   N8660.G64O9813 2004
   759.9492--dc22   2004043527

Designed by Patricia Fabricant

Printed in the United States

Frontispiece: Vincent van Gogh, *Cypresses with Two Women in the
Foreground*, 1889. Kröller-Müller Museum, Otterlo

CONTENTS

PREFACE

Amsterdam, Van Gogh Museum, December 1997

MY ENCOUNTER WITH THEO BEGAN WITH A MISTAKE.

I first met Theo's gaze one snowy afternoon on a trip to The Netherlands for the Christmas holiday. It was a lively, light-filled gaze, caught for posterity on the yellowed paper of a black-and-white photograph hanging on the wall of this fascinating museum.

As well acquainted with Vincent's work as I was, I thought that this was the master himself. The photograph showed a young man barely in his thirties, with delicate features and sporting a thick moustache. I was intrigued by his gentle expression, a world away from his tormented self-portraits. I knew—as many others do as well—the dark side of the famous painter so I was surprised by the brightness of the image. When would he ever have looked so radiant? Upon checking the photograph's caption, it proved to be not Vincent, but the other van Gogh, his brother Theo.

My interest was piqued: Who was this Theo? The holidays were over, but the memory of Theo's image stayed with me. Back in France—just out of curiosity—I wanted to know more. I returned to *Lettres de Vincent van Gogh à son frère Theo*, which I had abandoned in my library some time ago. The preface of this paperback edition, and the books I had on Vincent, fueled my interest in Theo. A host of questions remained unanswered. I also searched for a biography of him, in vain. There were none. It became clear to me that the thing to do was write one. A historian by training, I have always believed that individual lives are essential to an understanding of history. Biographies are very interesting to write, but necessarily entail lots of research. Knowing this, I discussed the idea at length with Frédérique de Jode, a friend since my college days. We had written together before, so that when I decided to undertake writing a biography about Theo it seemed perfectly natural to enlist her to take on the project with me. My enthusiasm was more than shared—it was doubled.

Marie-Angélique Ozanne

MARIE-ANGÉLIQUE'S ENTHUSIASM was indeed contagious. As soon as she suggested we write a biography of Theo van Gogh, I very much wanted to join her. We had met at the Sorbonne, where we were studying history, and later became colleagues when we both worked at the same newspaper. We had often talked about wanting to write a book together. Creating something together would represent a new phase in our collaboration and deepen our friendship.

The opportunity to write a series of portraits of contemporary artists for the newspaper *Quotidien de Paris* introduced us to fascinating artists of our own time. Theo and Vincent van Gogh offered a chance to learn more about another moment in art, which was undoubtedly one of the most important. Now it was my turn to plunge into Vincent's letters to Theo—such poignant writing, in which the artist told his closest confidant of his sorrows and joys—and the many biographies devoted to Vincent. As time went on, Theo claimed more and more of our time and our lives, and became the focus of our long conversations. Compelled to learn as much as we could about Theo, we spent days at a time doing research in the libraries of Paris trying to uncover his story. There was no denying my attachment to Theo. Although I admired his unfailing loyalty to his family, and his natural goodness, I also grieved to think how painful his life had been.

Frédérique de Jode

AFTER SCORES OF RESEARCH TRIPS and countless hours in libraries, we had an outline of Theo's brief life: a happy childhood; a tormented adolescence; a vow binding him to Vincent forever; a career as an art dealer in the service of the Impressionists; an unexpected love story with Johanna Bonger, his best friend's sister; the birth of his son, Vincent Willem; and an end, at thirty-three years old, as tragic as it was premature, only a few months after his brother's death. An enthralling life, with many gray areas remaining to be clarified.

With this short synopsis under our arm, we knocked at the doors of the publishing houses of Paris, urged on by our fierce desire to share this story. In every meeting, the publishers were similarly amazed. No biography of Theo van Gogh had ever been written, in any language, until now?

Theo is familiar to us as his Vincent's loyal younger brother in biographies on the painter and other books and articles that explored their complex relationship. To many, he was simply known as the recipient hundreds of Vincent's letters.

We wanted our biography to allow his voice to be heard. Once we had a signed contract with our original publisher, we asked the Fondation Vincent Van Gogh, of Amsterdam, which holds the family's private archives, to allow us to consult all documents concerning Theo, from his birth certificate to the medical report from the asylum where he died, and all the family's correspondence. Hundreds of letters traced every aspect of the family's history: the joys, dramas, and ordinary moments of everyday life. They were a long-winded family, accustomed to taking pen in hand to stay in touch with every member of the clan, wherever he or she might be. From concise notes to long missives from parents, brothers, and sisters, all the correspondence is indexed and numbered for the convenience of researchers. Contrary to what we expected, our access to the correspondence was limited by the language barrier—whether typewritten transcriptions or facsimiles of the original manuscripts, the letters are almost all in Dutch. Since neither of us speak the language, we turned to an exceptional translator, Ancilla Bossenec. We first heard of her when we were visiting Claude Millon, the author of *Vincent van Gogh à Auvers-sur-Oise*, a former schoolteacher who, in retirement, has become a specialist on the van Gogh family and a tireless lecturer in the city where the two brothers are buried. Claude, who was curious to know more about Theo, introduced us to Ancilla. Like any resident of Auvers, Ancilla, who is Dutch and married to a Frenchman, is well aware of the story of the van Goghs. Being involved herself in events relating to the Vincent, she was enthusiastic about our project. She was not with us on our first research trip to Amsterdam, so in Paris she translated orally the letters we brought back from the Fondation Vincent Van Gogh. We photocopied every single document that concerned Theo—a phenomenal number of letters. As it happened, to our great surprise, an international exhibition, *Theo Van Gogh: Art Dealer, Collector, Vincent's Brother*, was just then being mounted. The first major exhibition dedicated to Theo, it would inaugurate the reopening of Amsterdam's newly restored Van Gogh Museum before traveling to the Musée d'Orsay in Paris.

As Ancilla read, we would stop her at the passages that we needed for our work, and she would translate them in writing. Surprises emerged; for example, when we listened to the parents' voices in their letters to Theo, we heard how different the tone and content were from those in the letters to Vincent.

Before we left on a second research trip to Holland, our itinerary in France tracing following Theo's traces, took us from the usual places to unusual ones: museum libraries, Paris streets, the archives of the Paris hospitals and of the city of Auvers-sur-Oise, the Musée Goupil in Bordeaux, and Vincent's Provence.

En route to Amsterdam, we had to stop first in Brussels, where Theo made his debut as an art dealer, then in Zundert, his childhood home, and then in The Hague, where he experienced such a difficult period. Welcomed by Ancilla's Dutch family, we met up with our translator for more work sessions, this time on site, because the Fondation had given us permission to consult Theo and Johanna's correspondence, which was so valuable for our research. In his letters to his wife, Theo revealed himself as he had never done before. He opened up freely, expressing his torments, dreams, opinions, and above all his attachment to Vincent. Leaving Holland's grisaille behind us with our crucial documents in hand, we knew it was time to start writing. Through our pen, Theo would finally speak.

Marie-Angélique Ozanne and Frédérique de Jode
Paris, December 2003

INTRODUCTION

WOULD VINCENT HAVE BECOME VINCENT VAN GOGH without his brother Theo? Could he even have survived, let alone created, without the one who encouraged him, supported him—in every sense—and carried him through all the difficult years?

A number of Vincent's biographers, psychoanalysts and art historians alike, believe that he could never have become a painter without Theo. After all, it was Theo who urged him to become an artist, at a time when Vincent was at a crossroads in his life, and it was Theo who generously and continuously provided him with the means that made it possible for Vincent to devote himself exclusively to his life's work.

Theo van Gogh, Vincent's childhood playmate, became, over the years, his closest friend and confidant. Vincent's favorite brother acted as guide and benefactor within a complex and often times troubled relationship that would take him to the limits of his patience. In the end, Theo found himself as bound to Vincent as Vincent was to him.

Theo made possible Vincent's relatively small body of work—"made by the two of us," as Theo said. One brother painted, the other provided the means for him to pursue his passion without financial concerns.

Theo, a perceptive art dealer, supported the Impressionists and other avant-garde painters. Because he was cultured and discerning, he recognized their talent for what it was, and, in a lonely struggle, he attempted to promote it. Though his professional life was often troubled, he experienced real joy in his personal life when he married Johanna Bonger, who bore him a son, Vincent Willem. Despite this happiness, Theo's life was marred by tragedy—his brother's suicide being the most profound loss he would experience. Theo's short but singular life deserves to be known.

THEO | THE OTHER VAN GOGH

1 | A SHELTERED CHILDHOOD

1857-1870

T HE DESTINY OF THEO VAN GOGH—Vincent's soul
mate and brother—was inextricably rooted in
his family. He put his family first, and this was
the conviction that ultimately determined his actions, often at
the cost of agonizing sacrifices and much self-denial.

Theodorus, known as Theo, was born on May 1, 1857,
to a Calvinist family in Groot Zundert, a Catholic village of six
thousand in northern Brabant, on the Dutch-Belgian border.

His father, Pastor Theodorus (fig. 1), Dorus to the
family, had been officiating in Zundert for eight years. In
1851, thanks to matchmaking on the part of his brother Vincent, known as Cent (fig. 3), Dorus had married Anna Cornelia Carbentus (fig. 2), the daughter of a master bookbinder
at court and two and a half years older than Dorus.

Theo van Gogh at age 13

FIG. 1: *Theodorus van Gogh, 1822–1885, age 30*

FIG. 2: *Anna Cornelia van Gogh-Carbentus, 1819–1907*

They were a close and loving couple.

Traditionally, the van Goghs were either distinguished pastors or distinguished art dealers.[1] Theo's great-grandfather and grandfather, descendants from a line of gold-wire drawers in The Hague, were preachers. Three of his paternal uncles were wealthy dealers of prints and paintings.

Five years before Theo was born, a tragedy devastated Dorus and Anna. On March 30, 1852, their first son, named Vincent, was stillborn. One year later to the day after the traumatic event, Anna gave birth to another boy. The pastor and his wife agreed that he should be named Vincent, in memory of their first and in honor of Dorus's father and brother. By the time Theo came along, Vincent, born in 1853 (fig. 4), and a little girl, Anna (fig. 5), born in 1855, already shared the couple's peaceful life.

From their very first day together, a deep bond formed between this third child and his mother. No shadows of grief loomed over Dorus and Anna's infant boy. Unlike Vincent, fated to be born on a day of mourning, Theo awakened no painful memories. He was the much-anticipated son the family had long been waiting for.

Twenty-six years later, Dorus would write him: "We like to remember the day when you first came into the world. It was just like it was today. Extremely strong sunlight, a very cold east wind on the first day of the month of May. Dear Theo, for us you were like a spring flower that lasts a long time."[2]

Proud of his new son, this boy who bore his name, Dorus went in person to register the child at the Zundert town hall. On the following May 21, he would baptize Theo himself in the local church.

After Theo, three more children were born: Elisabeth (Lies), in 1859; Willemina (Wil), in 1862; and Cornelius

(Cor), in 1867 (figs. 6–8). Pa and Moe—as their children would always call them—raised their children in a small house in the center of town, on the street where the town hall and church were. The six children brightened the presbytery with their laughter and games. They grew up in cozy, though very modest, surroundings.

Anna and Dorus had little income. In 1871 a preacher earned eight hundred florins a year, plus an allowance of fifty florins paid by the Protestant community. To bring in something extra, Anna sometimes sold fruit from her orchard. Al-

Fig. 3: *Vincent van Gogh (known as Cent), 1789–1874*

though the van Gogh family lived very simply, they enjoyed the significant benefit of a servant and a governess, both of whom lived in—an unusual circumstance in the countryside at the time.

The village considered the family cultivated, oblig- ing, and respectable. The reverend and his wife enjoyed an excellent reputation; the community, Catholics and Protes- tants alike, praised them for their good hearts and their willingness to help the poor. Dorus, a handsome man with regular features and a gentle voice, visited his parish regu- larly, traveling from farm to farm to visit the sick. He also spent a great deal of time at the presbytery studying the Bible, which he would memorize in order to quote it to his

FIG. 4: *Vincent van Gogh, 1853–1890*

CLOCKWISE FROM TOP LEFT
FIG. 5: *Anna Cornelia van Gogh, 1855–1930*
FIG. 6: *Elisabeth Huberta (Lies) van Gogh, 1859–1936*
FIG. 7: *Willemina Jacoba (Wil) van Gogh, 1862–1941*
FIG. 8: *Cornelius Vincent (Cor) van Gogh, 1867–1900*

congregation or his children. He was a modest preacher, who served his church with sincerity and devotion. Unfortunately, however, he was also a terrible speaker, who had to work very hard to prepare his Sunday services. No one was allowed to disturb him during the long hours he spent studying alone in his office.

After work, "the handsome dominie," as his Protestant congregation called him,[3] would take his wife and children walking in the country for at least an hour.[4] At the end of the village were a pine forest and heather-covered slopes. All around, fields of rye and wheat extended as far as the eye could see. The river called to the boys, who loved to go fishing together. To an outsider, that gray, sandy, harsh landscape was the very picture of desolation, but for Vincent and Theo those energizing outings remained cherished memories throughout their lives. They continued the tradition of long walks when they were older; even when he was terribly busy, Theo would always manage to make time for them.

Dorus also saw to his children's religious education. Two paternal aunts gave them group catechism lessons. Their father inculcated in them Christianity's three theological virtues—faith, hope, and charity. A voracious reader himself, he introduced his children to literature that glorified their faith or presented a biblical morality. The love of books they received in early childhood would endure their entire lives.

As for Anna, she naturally took on the material, day-to-day concerns of a large family. Dignified despite the lack of money, she never let her worries about finances show. It was a typical marriage of the time: her husband was the authority figure and she carried out his decisions.

Like any pastor's wife, however, Anna was her husband's right hand. She took this mission very seriously, spending a great deal of time outside the house helping those who could not help themselves, and collecting food and clothing for the poor, regardless of religious persuasion.

Her maternal qualities were not restricted to her children. She never forgot that her religion preached generosity; she often reminded the children of this and repeatedly told them it would be disgraceful to reproach their mother for going out so much, when there were unfortunate people who needed her. For the people of the village, Anna was the very image of altruism, but her children often missed her.

Gentleness was the dominant feature of her complex personality, yet her sudden rages were legendary. Her friends found her "easy to get along with,"[5] but there was no contradicting her, for fear of arousing that infamous anger. This duality in her character would create problems later on in her adult sons' relationships with women.

After attending to her charity work, Anna looked after her children, imbuing them with a profound appreciation for nature, drawing, and the art of letter-writing, all of which would remain important to them throughout their lives.

When Anna was busy with other activities, she had the benefit of a governess who took over for her. (During his childhood, four different young women were responsible for Theo.)

Everything appeared to conspire to make Theo's early years a nurtured, even sheltered childhood. Unlike his older brother and sister, Vincent and Anna, he did not attend the Zundert school. There were two reasons for this: first, because Dorus intensely disliked the teacher, a notorious alcoholic, and second, because Dorus and Anna did not want to risk their children being influenced by the ignorant, brawling bumpkins in his class.

Nevertheless, the van Gogh children were not isolated: neighbors of the Honcoop brothers, the sons of a servant who had worked for the family for eighteen months, came regularly to play with them. At the same time, the pastor's children were more coddled than their playmates, even overprotected. Not sending them to school meant, in the end, depriving them of a kind of real experience of interacting with others, situations that sooner or later they would have to experience.

Physically, Theo was the image of his uncle Cent, his father's favorite brother: the same wavy hair and light eyes that softened a thin face. Nothing presaged his future delicate health. As one Zunderter attested, "Theo was stronger, taller, and slimmer than Vincent, and also noisier and more talkative."[6] In adolescence, each would acquire the other's physical qualities.

Theo was a lively but well-behaved child. The family saw Anna in Vincent and Dorus in Theo; Theo was generous, ready to help, and conciliatory, as well as timid and patient. He was a pleasant child, betraying no hint of rebelliousness. Theo was a peacemaker; in the face of any frustration or conflict, he internalized everything rather than initiate a confrontation—oftentimes at the cost of his own interests. He tried to make everyone happy, and wanted desprately not to disappoint anyone.

EVERY MORNING, Theo awoke in the family's pretty, two-story, typical Dutch-style house, which was surrounded by a garden. In her memoirs, Elisabeth fondly remembers beds of marigolds, mignonettes, and bright red geraniums.[7] Sometimes the drying laundry was laid out on the lawn to be bleached by the sun. In one corner, berry bushes aroused the gluttony of six little scapegraces. Elisabeth describes a harmony among the siblings—except for Vincent, who, even as a young child, tended to be a bit of a loner.

Because there was not enough room indoors, the van Gogh children made the garden their playground. One of their favorite pastimes was to slide down a small knoll; this always evoked happy shrieks and giggles. Elisabeth gives detailed accounts of their walks in the surrounding countryside, under the watchful eyes of their ever-protective parents. "Don't get too close to the river," they always warned.

Vincent was four years old when Theo was born. Like many elder children, he felt a mix of tenderness and jealousy upon first seeing the newborn. Yet a special bond soon formed between the two brothers. In Vincent biographer Marc Edo Tralbaut's view, Theo's birth somewhat assuaged Vincent's feelings of guilt about the death of the first baby, whom he vaguely felt he had "replaced."[8] This relief would have given rise to an extreme sense of gratitude toward the brother who had, in some sense, set Vincent free. This feeling underlaid the extraordinary friendship that connected the brothers for a lifetime.

Taking his role as elder brother seriously, Vincent took Theo under his wing, teaching him games and the joys of nature. Together, they built sandcastles. But it was not only Vincent who showered Theo with attention—his parents, brothers, and sisters were also affectionate. Vincent would later tease him about this, calling him "Lucky Theo."

Theo heeded and admired Vincent. Both brothers would look back at their childhood as a time of happiness, a sort of paradise lost, redolent of a child's freedom from worry. Years later, when Vincent was suffering terribly, he recalled to Theo: "During my illness I saw again every room of the house at Zundert, every path, every plant in the garden, the views from the fields round about, the neighbors, the graveyard, the church, our kitchen garden behind—down to the magpie's nest in a tall acacia in the graveyard."[9] And in another letter, overwhelmed by his affection for his childhood home, he exclaims: "O Zundert! Memories of you are sometimes almost overpowering."[10]

The First Separation

ON OCTOBER 1, 1864, Theo was separated from his favorite brother for the first time. Vincent was sent to Zevenbergen, to a boarding school run by Jean Provily. Theo envied his older brother the wonderful trip in a stagecoach with Dorus. As Theo watched his brother go, his brother was experiencing unbearable anxiety at the idea of being away from his family for so long.

At this time, Theo was only seven years old, and his lessons at home took up much of his day. Anna gave him valuable counsel, and encouraged and pampered him. He was now the only boy in the house.[11] He spent his days in an almost entirely female environment, and found that playing with his two little sisters was much less fun than playing with his inventive and resourceful older brother. Anna and the governess tried as best they could to fill the void, but Theo missed his brother.

Vincent received permission to spend the Christmas vacation at home. Everyone was glad to be together again, for as long as the school holidays allowed, and the two brothers were as close as ever.

In the 1866 school year, Vincent was enrolled at the Hannik Institute in Tilburg. After elementary school, he attended the William II, King of Holland, royal high school. Eventually, Theo became accustomed to his brother's absence, and though he missed him, his sadness was nothing like Vincent's wrenching distress—he experienced his separation from his family as a punishment he had done nothing to deserve. He did not understand his parents' decisions, and could not understand how these decisions would serve him in the future. Theo's, on the other hand, was a passing sorrow, soon forgotten in the comfort of his mother's arms.

And yet, Vincent enjoyed privileges that, for financial reasons, his younger brothers and sisters would not. When it was his turn, Theo would not receive the education Vincent did. Vincent and Theo's parents invested a great deal in Vincent's studies and his future success, perhaps in the hope that they might be able to make up to him for their very modest lifestyle.

A curious incident took place in the middle of 1868; Vincent mysteriously went back home to Zundert without finishing his last trimester at school. Although the painter's biographers have investigated the question at length, they have not discovered the reason for his early return—neither poor grades, nor questionable behavior, nor lack of money on his parents' part seems to account for it. Whatever the reason, when Vincent went home, no one took charge of organizing his intellectual activities. Anna was much too busy, and so Vincent idled his days away.

Meanwhile, Theo was still studying at the presbytery. He had obligations, and could not get away to keep his brother company. He could only watch him wander around aimlessly. The difference in their ages meant more now than in the past: at eleven, Theo was still a child, but, at fifteen,

Vincent was beginning to know the torments of adolescence.

When Vincent was old enough to work, it became imperative to find him a job that would allow him to help the family, or at least relieve some of their financial burden.

The family's straitened circumstances were nothing new. The rest of his family considered Dorus—who was content to live on the modest salary of a simple country preacher—poverty-stricken. Dorus had chosen a peaceful, hard-working life, with neither pomp nor weighty responsibilities. But he still had to meet his family's everyday needs.

Dorus's world was a contemplative one, removed from the realities of life. The outside world failed to hold his attention, whether it was the death of the Netherlandish king, William II, in 1849; the series of revolutions that were shaking the realm; or the religious and educational questions that were dividing the nation. Even the abolition of slavery, in 1860, seems not to have caught his attention. The van Goghs lived in isolation, entirely taken up with their children, parish, and family.

Fortunately, Cent, a successful art dealer, helped his brother Dorus financially. Being childless, he was very devoted to his nieces and nephews. However, their rich uncle's condescension toward the father they admired made Theo and his siblings uncomfortable. They felt humiliated by their financial distress and by their father's attitude of dependence toward his relatives, especially Cent. Dorus never asked for help, but his father's financial inferiority was not lost on the young Theo, whose sensitive nature was bruised by it.

Cent found a way to get Vincent a job: the old dealer was tired, and had for some time been thinking of retiring. He sold his gallery in The Hague to Goupil, the famous art dealer, who was his associate in Paris. Cent's dream was for his nephew to take up the torch. Vincent would, of course, start at the bottom of the ladder as a a mere apprentice, like all the employees of Goupil & Cie. An agreement was soon reached, to everyone's satisfaction.

Dorus was planning to move his family to Helvoirt, another town in the region of Brabant. After twenty years of good and loyal service to Zundert, he received an offer to transfer. Strangely, the appointment did not represent a promotion, even though the pastor's salary would be higher. Dorus accepted, because their expenses were about to increase: Anna and Theo would be going to boarding school, and Dorus would soon have to pay the fee to exempt the boys from military service.

On January 29, 1871, Dorus preached his last sermon to his congregation, who were visibly moved. It was time for the van Goghs to pack up and say their farewells to the Zundert community. This page of Theo's childhood was turning.

2 A SACRIFICED ADOLESCENCE

1871-1878

O N JANUARY 31, Dorus, Anna, the children, and their governess moved into the Helvoirt presbytery. They were greeted by a new home, surrounded by a flower garden and with an orchard and kitchen garden, all white with winter frost. Before long, the family had unpacked their trunks and brought life and warmth into their new home, and gotten their bearings before the official reception. Dorus apprehensively prepared his entrance.

The much-anticipated event took place on February 5. The village's Protestant community turned out in its Sunday best, and hurried to see the new pastor and, incidentally, hear his sermon. His audience seemed won over, an impression that subsequent events would confirm. At the time of

Theo at age 21

Dorus's arrival, his parish numbered only sixty congregants, and Helvoirt's poor church was in such pitiful condition that he would have to ask the board of the Dutch church for special funds to restore it. Work on the church began in September of the following year, just in time to keep the building from collapsing. To the great joy of the pastor and his wife, attendance began to increase steadily. The van Goghs' devotion animated the parish's religious life, in part because the reverend and his family spared no effort to win the parishioners over. Anna started a school to teach sewing and knitting. Theo, too, performed charitable works, such as regularly visiting the orphanage at Buren, where he formed a friendship with a young girl who lived there.[1]

At the same time, he was attending classes in French, English, German, mathematics, and drawing in the neighboring town of Oisterwijk. Ted—as the village children had nicknamed him[2]—was attending school for the first time. It was a private school founded in 1862 that took only Protestant day students and boarders. Every day, Theo set out with his pal Constant for the two-hour walk.

When summer vacation rolled around, Theo couldn't wait to see Vincent, who was just as glad to leave The Hague, the Goupil gallery, and his friends to spend the holidays with his family. Theo was anxious to hear his older brother's impressions of city life. Would he still be the same after the long months apart? The intimacy between the two brothers was instantly rekindled. As always, they went off by themselves, walking for hours in the countryside. It was agreed that when Vincent left to return to The Hague at the end of August, Theo would go with him and stay a few days. For the first time, Vincent and Theo were alone together outside the family circle and both were very excited about it. Theo shared

Vincent's room at the Rooses, a boardinghouse only minutes from the center of town.

Theo was in awe of his brother, who was strong physically, whereas thin, long-limbed Theo appeared sickly. Vincent acted as mentor and was perfectly delighted with this role. During this period, Vincent projected the manner of someone who takes everything in stride, while Theo was already the thwarted-dreamer type. He took his brother's advice and admired his learned and mature posture.

One afternoon, they started out on a ramble toward the farther outskirts of the city. Surprised by a rainstorm, they arrived soaking wet at the Rijswijk mill, where they took refuge, and gulped down a delicious glass of milk. Compelled by the emotion of the moment, they swore always to be there for each other, regardless of whatever circumstances or distance might come between them. In Vincent's letters, he refers to the event as an extraordinary moment: "That Rijswijk road holds memories for me which are perhaps the most beautiful I have . . ."[3] To ensure that Theo would forever remember that poignant day, Vincent sent him a reproduction of a painting of the mill by Johannes Hendrik Weissenbruch, and often urged him to maintain and foster the feeling that connected the two of them.

Theo returned to Helvoirt with his head full of images from his visit. When he writes his brother to thank him for those magnificent days, Vincent writes back: " . . . I was glad to hear you arrived home safely. I missed you the first few days and it felt strange not to find you there when I came home in the afternoons."[4]

This was the beginning of the extraordinary correspondence between the two brothers, which only ended with Vincent's death in 1890. Commencing on that August day of

1872, Theo would keep every one of his brother's letters as if it were a holy relic. (Theo's first letters to his brother, on the other hand, have never been found, except for one dated September 7, 1875, with Vincent's reply on the back.)

LIFE RETURNED TO NORMAL. Every day until December, there were classes, homework, pastoral duties, and, above all, the difficult road to Oisterwijk. Vincent commiserated with his brother for the long daily trek in the snow and cold.

At Christmas, the family joyfully reunited in Helvoirt. Anna prepared the Christmas tree and decorations, which, like every year, enchanted the young children of the village. And yet, the atmosphere was less lighthearted than usual. An air of melancholy pervaded the house: after the holidays, Theo would be leaving.

The van Goghs' financial difficulties were getting worse. Besides Theo's schooling, the pastor was paying for Anna's foreign-language classes at a school in Leeuwarden. He also anticipated the extraordinary expense of 625 florins to save his three sons from military service.[5] This represented an astronomical sum in terms of the household income. Fifteen-year-old Theo would have to go to work. His uncle Cent was immediately consulted. Prompted by the gallery director's complimentary remarks about Vincent, Cent was happy to see to it that Theo was hired at the same firm.

Cent and the Art Business

CENT WAS TWO YEARS OLDER THAN DORUS. The two brothers further enhanced their close relationship by marrying two sisters. Unfortunately, Cent and his wife remained childless, so he transferred his affection to his nieces and nephews, whom he spoiled at every possible opportunity.

Cent's health was poor, as a result of the scarlet fever he had contracted at twelve years old. Complications from that illness continued to plague him: he suffered, among other things, from severe migraine headaches. Though his physical condition had not prevented him from working, it had created considerable problems in both his private life and career.

Unable to follow any course of study consistently, he first tried to work in an office in Rotterdam, but his illness soon forced him to leave. A few years later, his cousin Hendrik van der Brugh, who owned a shop that sold artists' materials in The Hague, took him on as an assistant. Cent quickly proved himself—so much so that he took over the business from his cousin two years later and moved it to the Spuistraat, a more commercial area. His clients, who were mostly artists, eventually gave him the idea of also selling their work. Over the years, Cent made a name for himself as a connoisseur and businessman. In 1846 he made his first trip to Paris to keep up with what was happening in the art world. Beginning in 1851, the van Gogh name begins to appear in the ledgers of the Goupil gallery in Paris, a firm specializing in reproductions of paintings, old master prints, and of the work of contemporary artists exhibiting in the great Salons.

Cent, who was by now a respected art dealer, received a proposal from Goupil to form a partnership; he agreed and signed the deal in 1861. He moved to Paris, first to Rue Chaptal, then to an impressive town house in Neuilly. Cent and Dorus's brother Hendrik—known as Hein—took over the gallery in The Hague, which in time became Goupil's Dutch branch. Business between the galleries in Paris and in Holland grew at an extraordinary rate. At Cent's suggestion, Goupil mass-produced engravings after paintings. So successful was the venture that Cent was awarded the Dutch Order of the Oak Crown.

In 1871, Cent, now fifty-one years old and exhausted by illness, resigned from Goupil & Cie. in Paris. After ten years of a fruitful partnership, he continued his association with the French firm as a client. At the time that he was launching Theo into the art business, he was still on excellent terms with the old Adolphe Goupil, who was also gradually passing the torch to two other associates: Léon Boussod and his son-in-law, René Valadon.

Although the firm would become "Boussod and Valadon," it would always remain just "Goupil" to artists (fig. 1).

Because Vincent was employed in The Hague, it seemed inappropriate to hire his younger brother at the same branch. And since Theo had never been away from home, his parents did not want him too far away. Eventually he was placed in Brussels, at a gallery formerly run by his uncle Hein.

Fig. 1: *Boussod, Valadon & Cie's (Goupil & Cie.) in The Hague in 1898*

A New Life in Brussels

Hendrik Vincent van Gogh (1814–1877)—had begun his career as a bookseller. His first wife was Johanna Samuelle de Geus; they had a daughter, Elisabeth Huberta, in 1838. Sadly, Johanna died a year later. In 1841 Hein married his second wife Maria Boon. Then Hein fell sick with the chronic illness that was to torment him for the rest of his life. Beginning in 1858, he let his young associate run the business, and collaborated instead with his brother Cent in The Hague. Hein soon opened his own gallery in Brussels, which he sold off to Goupil, also for health reasons, in 1872, just before his nephew Theo arrived.

When Theo showed up for his first day of work at the Brussels gallery on January 6, it was managed by M. V. Schmidt, whom Vincent knew: "Father wrote me that you are on good terms with Mr. Schmidt; that is right—I think he is a good fellow from whom you can learn a great deal."[6]

The Goupil gallery in Brussels was on Rue de la Montagne-de-la-Cour. The art dealer with the last name of Bernheim was nearby. He was doing better than his competitors—the French firms were unable to get a firm foothold in Brussels. Goupil would close in 1880, and Durand-Ruel survived for only a year (1872–1873). There was one fundamental reason for these failures: the wealthy Brussels art collectors bought in Paris, where they lived for part of the year. At that time, the Belgian capital lacked Paris's imperial aura. It was still provincial in some ways, despite a policy of urban renewal that was sponsoring colossal works intended to give the city an international stature. The old, run-down Brussels was disappearing, however slowly, along with the nauseating stench of the Senne River, which would be vaulted over.

Belgium was a young nation, born in 1830 of a revolution fomented by the French-speaking, Catholic bourgeoisie against the Dutch Orange-Nassau rulers and their Protestant court. It was considered one of the most prosperous countries of Europe—in Brussels, running water was installed in doors in 1854, the sewer system was built between 1840 and 1870, and the grand avenues—undoubtedly inspired by Baron Haussmann's vision of Paris—were completed in 1871.

King Leopold II wished to see his kingdom's capital become modern and influential. The center of town became alive, and every cultural expression was fostered. French sculptors such as Albert-Ernest Carrier-Belleuse and Auguste Rodin were commissioned to decorate the facade of the Royal Conservatory of Music beginning in 1872.

Thus, when Theo arrived in Brussels he was coming into an environment where creativity and artistic expression were supported and encouraged. Artistically, the 1860s had witnessed the emergence of a new generation of painters who were breaking with the academy. The Société libre des beaux-arts—the Free Society of the Fine Arts—was fighting to have its kind of realism acknowledged. The group summed up its ambition in a single phrase: "The free, individual interpretation of nature."[7] The society rallied for most of the "landscape painters influenced by the Barbizon School and the social realists,"[8] such as Edmond Lambrichs, Eugène Smits, Alfred Verwée, Charles De Groux, Félicien Rops, Louis Dubois, Louis Artan, and Constantin Meunier. It organized exhibitions of paintings by Gustave Courbet, Charles-François Daubigny, Jean-François Millet, and Théodore Rousseau. Beginning in 1872, a magazine, L'Art libre, promulgated the ideas of this avant-garde group. The Brussels Goupil gallery showed the painters of the main Paris branch, but showed local artists, too.

Theo was amazed. He discovered painting the way some people undergo a religious conversion. He threw himself into this new world, with little regard for anything else. With both humility and passion he wanted to understand everything—the business, but also the art and the artists. Though he lacked self-confidence and self-assurance, he had a deep commitment. Vincent, his experienced guide, encouraged him to discover the artworks in museums, and writes his confidant, "I am very happy that you work in the same firm."[9] This new development brought the brothers even closer together; now they could talk about their common passion and begin a genuine epistolary exchange about art. Theo was captivated by the paintings of Alfred-Jean-André Cluysenaer, and by those of the celebrated Alfred Stevens, a Belgian-born painter and friend of Edouard Manet who lived in Paris. His Realist scenes of poverty did not sell very well, but his portraits of sophisticated women of the Second Empire had made him hugely successful.

The various Goupil galleries worked closely together, and this allowed Vincent and Theo to correspond via the packing crates for paintings that traveled between Brussels and The Hague. In his letters, Vincent asked his brother about the business: Did the Brussels gallery still have Vernier's Camille Corot album? Would Theo keep him informed about any innovations in etching and lithography, since these were not specialties of Vincent's branch?

Theo, too, asked technical questions, such as about photoengraving. He showed himself a curious and enthusiastic apprentice, fascinated by his work, and patient and dedicated. From the very beginning, his personality appealed to Schmidt, who became an encouraging professional mentor.

THEO STAYED IN A GOOD BOARDINGHOUSE on Rue du Marché-aux-herbes, in the center of town, a few minutes from the gallery. His hosts, the Van Brinks, a pastor and his wife, who gave him catechism lessons, were probably acquaintances of his uncle Hein. Hein was often ill, and so could not look after his nephew as he would have liked. Dutifully, Theo sometimes visited him on his days off, though he much preferred walking for hours on end down the alleys of the Bois, a favorite destination of the Bruxellois for their Sunday strolls. Even though he was thankful for some of the comforts he had, Theo's early days in Brussels were difficult.

Theo's mother wrote him often, sending him long, affectionate letters. Every piece of mail, besides local news and the inevitable observation on the importance of faith, brought Theo reminders of how happy his parents were that he was on this new path, and how much they missed him. "It is very strange here. To us, you are here, everywhere, all day long. Everyone speaks of you,"[10] Anna tells him. Dorus reveals a similar sentiment: "We never stop thinking of you, and it feels strange to us that you are gone."[11] Both address him as if he were a child thrust prematurely into an adult world. It had been different with Vincent, who went through all the various stages of childhood—boarding school, then high school—that prepare adolescents to live in society. His parents' choice to wean Theo more abruptly than his brother had left them feeling slightly guilty, so they gave him as much attention as they could.

Eventually, Theo more than adjusted to the city his brother called "pretty Brussels"—he came to love it. He perfected his French, which his mother urged him to speak often: " . . . that way, before you know it, you'll speak it as well as you do Dutch. And it won't have cost you anything."[12]

Money worries are a constant theme in his parents' letters. They appreciate Vincent's earning a living and help-ing the family. "[Vincent] is setting a good example for the others. I'd very much like to hear how it goes at the end of the month, and if you will be receiving something,"[13] Dorus inquires. Just a few weeks later he explodes with joy when Theo receives his first paycheck. "It is wonderful that you are working on your own. You can be useful and independent! It must give you a good feeling to receive your first thirty francs' salary. Now you will be able to help us. . . . So that I need pay only fifty francs instead of eighty every month. You can imag-ine how difficult things are for us at the moment."[14] He takes the opportunity to enumerate the household expenditures, from Anna's boarding fees (two hundred florins) to the smallest daily outlay (twenty-five florins), adding that his income is inadequate to cover their expenses and that he finds himself obliged to sell some personal items. Theo could not disappoint the family. It was imperative that he help them, since they considered him their godsend. To that end, he worked very hard. He got along well with Schmidt, and filled in capably for him when he went on vacation.

Nevertheless, his stay in Brussels ended in Novem-ber. When Vincent was transferred to London in May 1873, Dorus persuaded Cent that Theo should take his place in The Hague. A promising future lay ahead of him.

Theo was devastated by the news. He was finally en-joying the Belgian capital. The big-city atmosphere on a hu-man scale, and the artistic ferment at this crossroads between north and south, suited him very well; besides which, he had friends he had met in a young people's group.

The Gallery in The Hague

THEO ARRIVED IN THE HAGUE on November 12 with an excellent letter of recommendation from his employer in his pocket.[15] He knew the city from his brief stay with Vincent in August 1872. At the time, the royal capital was a charming city surrounded by forests. It was peaceful and elegant, and home to a circle of intellectuals and artists.

As Vincent had done, Theo boarded with the Rooses, a pleasant, bourgeois family with no intellectual pretensions, who lived in a small, quiet neighborhood not far from the center of town. The rent was reasonable.

Because Anna was originally from The Hague, Theo had family there. He was a regular visitor at the home of his aunt Fie—who had married Anna's brother, Arie Carbentus—and her three daughters, but his close friends were Annette and Caroline Haanebeek, his cousins by marriage. According to the historian Elly Cassee, Vincent had been secretly in love with Caroline, and Theo with Annette,[16] ever since their teenage years. According to Cassee, ever since the fateful walk to the Rijswijk mill, the brothers had exchanged confidences about the feelings they shared for the two sisters. With the example of their parents before them—two brothers who married two sisters—they imagined themselves becoming "brothers twice over." Their plans were dashed, however, when Caroline married another man in the spring of 1871.

Theo often saw Annette, her parents, and the young married couple, and enjoyed conversations with them that were more intellectual than those with the Rooses.

Professionally, Theo was very busy; his work at the Goupil gallery took up a great deal of his time. As soon as he arrived, his employer, Hermanus Gijsbertus Tersteeg (fig. 2), sent him on a trip to Utrecht. As agreed, Theo more or less filled the position of clerk left vacant by Vincent, who had also been in charge of the department of photographic reproductions. In a letter to Theo, he declared that he had made as many as one hundred sales a day. In the beginning, Theo's tasks as a clerk were many and varied: packing and unpacking canvases, preparing orders, and sometimes giving a client information. Theo learned the trade and discovered genuine works of art, many still redolent of turpentine and fresh varnish, straight from the artists' studios.

Theo's worked under Tersteeg, the twenty-eight-year-old director, who had made his name as an importer of English-language books to Amsterdam, before he was spotted by Cent van Gogh. This brilliant young man, a passionate lover of books, had been a bookseller and lecturer before embarking upon a promising career in the art business. Because Theo was Cent's nephew and Vincent's brother, Tersteeg took him under his wing. The director, who with his wife and daughter, lived in an apartment over the gallery, invited his employees to drop by. Vincent urged his brother to do so, but Theo was too shy. Paralyzed by the curse of his timidity, he felt uncomfortable in foreign territory.

At sixteen, he was still a reserved, even self-effacing, uncomplicated young man, still constantly and conscientiously aware of his parents' advice and ambitions for him. They wanted him to make a good impression, and told him more than once, "Be sure always to dress well, especially at the gallery. You can never be too careful about that. We can help you if you need something. You must always be a gentleman, and not a servant."[17] They dreamed of turning their son into a man who would be respected and admired in society, much like Cent and the gallery's rich clients.

And indeed the Goupil branch was patronized by wealthy, sophisticated art lovers, who expected a reception worthy of their standing. The gallery was composed of a series of rooms with a rich and opulent décor: there were velvet sofas, heavy drapes, and costly display cabinets; ostentatiously framed paintings adorned the walls. Theo was well aware of his good fortune, and proud to work in an environment that allowed him to admire and meet fashionable artists, such as Jacobus Maris and Anton Mauve. Vincent, on the other hand, had very eclectic tastes—a list he made up was as diverse and incongruous as a post-mortem inventory.[18]

Fig. 2: *Hermanus Gijsbertus Tersteeg*

The choices that Theo made in those early years as an apprentice appear more considered than his brother's. He steadily developed his eye, and complemented his training by reading art periodicals and books, as well as with visits to nearby museums, such as the Mauritshuis, with its collections of Brueghels, Rembrandts, Rubenses, Van Ruysdaels, and Vermeers. Vincent complimented his work: "I know you are doing well at The Hague, because Mr. Tersteeg told me so. I can see from your letter that you are taking a keen interest in art, and that's a good thing, old fellow. I'm glad you like Millet, Jacque, Schreyer, Lambinet, Frans Hals, etc."[19]

Frans Hals belonged to the School of The Hague, one of the collections that had made the gallery's reputation. One early-twentieth-century observer, commenting on the best art dealers in the Netherlands, noted: "I must honestly say that Goupil, in the person of its director, Mr. Tersteeg, made the least good impression on me—Van Wisselingh's judgment was more assured, Cor van Gogh's more sophisticated. Nevertheless, its actions and activity make the firm of Goupil et Cie of The Hague more important, when it comes to the history of the School of The Hague."[20]

A contemporary school, founded by Johannes Bosboom and whose leading exponent was Josef Israëls, had been revising the concept of landscape painting in Holland since the early 1870s. Several painters of the group who had trained in Paris or Brussels—Hendrik Mesdag, Mauve, and Maris—had set up their easels in Scheveningen, a well-known seaside resort. The best of the group, Hendrik Weissenbruch, painted urban and rural scenes. In his work created before 1875, he scrupulously rendered every detail; after, he favored simple, rapid brushstrokes.

Like Cent, Tersteeg was able to attract many artists, whom he signed up with the gallery. The queen herself, as well as the great Dutch collectors, came to the gallery to commission the works of these artists, who became quite successful. Local artists frequented the gallery in order to discover or revisit the masters of the Barbizon School. Vincent and Theo met Mauve, who was fascinated by Millet's work, thanks to reproductions sold by Goupil. Mauve became a member of the van Gogh family on November 26, 1874, when he married Ariëtte Sophia Jeannette Carbentus, nicknamed Jet, a cousin of the two brothers.

Financially, Theo was doing well; his first sortie was promising, and he was earning a respectable living, although his salary did not yet allow him to be independent. His father reassures him: "If you need anything after you've used up your salary, I'll make up the difference for your expenses. . . . You know you must be frugal and always think before spending, but whatever you need, we will provide." He then adds: "I think it's really wonderful that you are already earning so well. . . . We know that you are already doing your part to alleviate our worries and be our joy. . . . My dear Theo, even though you are far away, you know very well that you are our pride and joy."[21]

On a material level, everything was going well, but Theo was sliding into depression. His young life seemed to be slipping away from him. He liked his work, he had a wide circle of friends, yet he was plagued by worry. It seemed a serious depression was brewing.

He sorely missed the peace of his childhood, and was troubled by the heat of his sexual desires. But to whom could he turn? The van Goghs did not talk about such things. Sex was mythified—sublimated—until marriage. Religious education and modesty alike imposed silence. It is very likely that Theo had been frequenting a brothel since 1874. The Hague's red-light district was also the painters' quarter. There, as elsewhere, prostitutes frequently initiated minors, often schoolboys. When he could stand it no longer, Theo confessed his dalliances to his brother, describing the atmosphere of pleasure and debauchery, revealing his desire and his shame.

Vincent was not understanding. Steeped in an exalted religiosity, he replies: "'Ye judge after the flesh; I judge no man.' 'He that is without sin among you, let him cast a stone at her.' So keep to your own ideas, and if you doubt whether they are right, test them with those of Him who dared to say, 'I am the truth,' or with those of some very human person, Michelet, for instance. . . . Virginity of soul and impurity of body can go together."[22] Theo was bitterly disappointed. The intimacy between the brothers waned, and after Vincent's letter their correspondence stopped for the first time, and would not resume until February 1875.

What Theo did not know was that this was an unfortunate time to look to Vincent for sympathy, who had just been rebuffed. Eugenie Loyer, the daughter of his London landlady, had rejected him. He persisted silently and stubbornly, convinced that the high-mindedness of his sentiments would eventually win the girl over. But Vincent's was an imaginary, unreciprocated passion, and Eugenie never gave in. In his letters, Vincent never reveals his intense feelings for this woman. Prudish and private, he kept to lectures on painting or literature; during this period, the tone of his letters becomes slightly pedantic and condescending toward his brother. Vincent wrote Theo about Michelet—not about the great works of the historian of the French Revolution, but about a small treatise, *L'Amour*, a naïve glorification of the ideal, well-behaved wife. Otherwise, Vincent hid behind his Bible, at a time when he, too, was undergoing a difficult period concerning love and sex.

It was clear to his parents when they saw him over the holidays that the atmosphere of the Loyer family in London was not good for Vincent. They decided that Vincent would return with his sister Anna, who was looking for a position as a tutor abroad. Brother and sister eventually moved to a new rooming house, which was a relief to their mother.

For a few weeks, Vincent was enjoying life again thanks to Anna's warmth. Then, after his sister found a position, he sank into a depression once more, finding some small comfort in his liturgical readings and in drawing, which he had practiced virtually uninterrupted since childhood. His employer, Obach, became aware of his employee's mental distress and lack of interest in his work. Seriously concerned, he told Cent. They came to the conclusion that London's climate was bad for Vincent. He would be transferred to Paris immediately, so that his spirits would improve, along with his inclination for the art business. Although the French capital had made a strong impression on Vincent when he had spent a few days there in May 1873, this time, his family's unquestioned assumption that they had a right to make decisions about his life exasperated him. He suspected his father of having a part in Cent's requesting his transfer. He was so angry that he decided to cut off all correspondence with his family in Holland. Dorus and Anna were terribly upset by this, and assured Theo that they had not, as Vincent believed, initiated such a request. Dorus writes: "Dear Theo, Your most recent letter gives me the opportunity to come back to a passage in it. I am not planning to ask for a transfer for Vincent. I don't want to take on such a responsibility. . . . I think we should stick to letting Uncle Cent take care of your and your brother's affairs."[23] Theo tried to keep things in perspective. But on November 18, 1874, Anna writes: "My dear Theo, It is lovely to hear from you, and really it's very sweet of you to want to cheer us up. We wish we could be cheerier. You say: Now, things are going well, and we must look on the bright side . . . but you also say we shouldn't worry so much, that it makes us unhappy. My dear child, a father and mother's happiness depends on their children's. Have you written him? If not, do so again. He loves you so much!"[24]

Vincent, however, was just as uncommunicative with Theo as he was with his parents. A letter from Anna tells Theo that, finally, on November 20, Vincent had decided to send them "some news," and that on November 25 he had sent them "a little twenty-franc note, without a word." On December 14, another letter from Vincent to his parents was received. Anna was delighted. By mid-December, their worry seems to have dissipated. Vincent told his parents that he would come to Helvoirt for Christmas. They could hardly wait to see him, and prayed that his plans would not be thwarted at the last minute. Theo, too, was giving them cause for concern. While Vincent was finding passages in the Bible that eased his pain, Theo was expressing grave doubts about religion. Nonetheless, he accepted, more or less under duress, to make his profession of faith on December 26, 1874, during the Christmas celebrations, even though the prospect of the sacrament did not satisfy his innermost questions.

Since 1873, Dorus and Anna had had to exhort him to go to church. They regularly asked him how his catechesis was going and if he was keeping it up. Since arriving in The Hague, he had been halfheartedly attending Reverend Van der Broeke's dreary class. On September 2, 1874, his father queries him yet again: "How is the catechism going? You are attending regularly, aren't you, and church, too? I would think you'd have your pick in The Hague." On October 28, Dorus was more deeply troubled about Theo's uncertainties. Apparently, Theo had asked whether it was really necessary to attend church, whether nature did not evoke God better than preachers and their sermons. Both his parents responded to this. Anna writes: "Dear child, You ask our opinion. Whether nature is all a man needs. Nature without the Bible is the way of the pagans, and we know how far they are. . . . You, however, speak of nature without church, but with the Bible. Except that nature doesn't speak of Jesus, and he is the one who really brings us the true enjoyment of nature, for he is the one who . . . arranges our destiny, the same way he tends nature. This father has good will toward you, even if you have not had good will toward him. And that's why Jesus speaks of forgiveness and makes us happy forever."[25] Her arguments, as inspired as they were, did not appease Theo. And Dorus adds: "My son, you, too, need faith. Need to believe. Need religion. I know it, and you feel it. But there is an obstacle that has tripped up many people."[26] The obstacle was that Theo was tired of all these religious arguments, which were a world away from the philosophers he was discovering. He was no longer a well-behaved child, keeping his notions to himself. "Your father would like to come across, not as an old idiot, but as an understanding friend. I was once young, too," Dorus writes. Despite all the pastor's good will, Theo was losing his bearings; he no longer knew where he stood.

Christmas 1874 brought the family together; it had been two years since Vincent and Theo had seen each other. Even though they had both spent the summer holidays at Helvoirt, they had visited their parents in turn, and so missed each other. In this last week of the year, Theo would be confirmed, despite his reservations, and Vincent would again grow close to his family.

1875: A Difficult Year

A FEW MONTHS LATER, a tragic event fueled Theo's doubts. On June 14, 1875, Annette Haanebeek died of an incurable illness at twenty-four years of age. Theo had enjoyed her family's company ever since he moved to The Hague, so much so that he saw her almost exclusively. His parents approved of their relationship, but also encouraged him to have others, perhaps suspecting their son's feelings for his distant cousin.

When Annette, still so young, told him her fate was sealed, Theo no longer knew which way to turn. The woman he had dreamed of marrying was gone before he was even able to contemplate declaring his intentions. He sank gradually into a depression his parents had never seen before. For the first time, Dorus and Anna felt genuinely helpless. Dorus, already saddened by Vincent's depression, pleads with Theo to pull himself together: "Melancholy can be harmful, and to indulge in melancholy does not help to produce energy. My dear Theo! You should really think about that; I see that recently your liveliness has diminished, your cheerfulness is no longer what it was before. . . . Am I mistaken? Is there something I can do to cheer you up?"[27] Hoping to reach his son, he quotes one of his favorite authors: "Michelet says that a bird must help his babies from his experience. He warns them, gives them information, encourages them. But we do that, too."[28] Dorus asks Theo to keep his letter, which displays a fatherly sensitivity and compassion.

Vincent, who had resumed his correspondence with his brother, also tried to help him, but his remedy was always the same—the Bible. Theo and Vincent grew closer, but when Annette fell ill, Theo said nothing about it to his confidant. It was Dorus who told Vincent, who was unaware the situation was grave. On June 19, 1875, he writes Theo from Paris: "I had hoped to revisit her before her death, but it was not to have been. *L'homme s'agite et Dieu le mène* [Man proposes and God disposes]."[29] This is a rather glib statement concerning the woman who had been the love of Theo's youth. Vincent adds in a postscript: "You will certainly not forget her, or her death, but it is better to keep that to yourself. It is one of those things that, as time goes by, we 'are sorrowful but always rejoicing'; that is what we have to learn."[30] Keep the problem a secret, hide your feelings, act as if the world hasn't crumbled— Vincent had taken the family lesson to heart. As for Theo, he did not answer Vincent's letter, and closed himself firmly within his sorrow.

At first, Vincent thought a change of scene would be the best thing for his brother. He asked Theo directly about this, and began working out a plan to have him transferred to London or Paris. Theo would have liked to leave The Hague. Though Cent was told this, nothing came of it. On the one hand, Tersteeg was very satisfied with Theo's work, and on the other Vincent's chopping and changing had not produced any good results. Beginning on July 24, Vincent changed his mind and started constantly encouraging his brother to go out, not to shut himself up in his unbearable loneliness. At the same time, Vincent was still quoting passages from the Bible or from sermons that he had piously attended. Despite his increasing doubts, Theo had not yet conclusively broken with religion. Among other evidence of this is the fact that he copied out poems inspired by the Gospel for his sister, who thanked him warmly. In a letter of September 7, 1875, which, unusually, has survived, Theo admits to Vincent that he went to church to hear "a beautiful sermon. Jesus wept," and mentions his roommate, Johannes Wilhelmus Weehuyzen, who also died recently, and with whom Theo had had long discussions about Michelet's *L'Amour*.[31] Vincent's reply is chilling: "Keep your eyes open, and try to be strong and brave."[32] He went on to advise Theo firmly to get rid of the book and read only the Bible. He could not bear what he perceived as Theo's indulging his ineffable pain, resorting to the church only to ease his melancholy. It exasperated Vincent to see Theo surrender to his malaise, and spend his time reading and copying the works of the German poet Friedrich Rückert. To Theo, the verses of *Childhood Memories of a Village Civil Servant's Son* recalled the happy days in Zundert, while the sonnets of the *Funeral Verses for Agnes* let him weep for a love that was lost before it even really existed— Annette. Although Vincent was not very well himself, he worried about his younger brother's health, urging Theo to eat properly, develop a strong body, and maintain faith in the future: "It is sometimes necessary 'not to dream, not to sigh.'"[33] And in the next letter he writes: "Courage, old son, after the rain, good weather: keep hoping for that."[34]

Vincent looked forward impatiently to the Christmas holidays, when he would see his brother and the rest of the family. Theo, too, could hardly wait to see them. The year 1875 had been an especially trying one for him. At eighteen years old he felt weak and worn out. His body manifested his moral malaise: he had lost his appetite and hurt his foot in a fall, and was suffering from toothaches. Differences of opinion with his employer were vexing him, as two letters show. One is from Laurent Vink, a friend, who encourages him not to allow himself to be taken advantage of: "I learned from Willem that your boss is absolutely putting one over on you. You must tell him how mine is about vacations. Maybe that'll influence that barbarian a little."[35] The other is from Vincent: "Above all, save some love for the business and for your work, and respect for Mr. Tersteeg. One day you will appreciate, better than now, how much he deserves it. No need to overdo it, though."[36]

Adding to Theo's professional troubles were the deaths of two other people close to him: Jan Carbentus, one of his uncles, and one of Theo's dearest friends, young Willem Laurens Khiel, who also lived at the Rooses'. Theo was shattered by this double bereavement. His father tried to comfort him by reminding him that Christians believe in eternal life, which is better in every way than the earthly life. Theo's mother and sister also sustained him with their letters. His family's solicitude was as precious to him as it was at times suffocating. The Christmas holidays represented hope: they would all be together again, warmly reassembling their close family, though not at Helvoirt.

Dorus had changed parishes. At the suggestion of his superiors in the church, and after visiting Etten, a village with a Protestant community of about 120 people, and taking the financial aspects into consideration, Dorus agreed to become the new pastor. On October 17, 1875, he preached his farewell sermon in Helvoirt to a congregation saddened by his imminent departure. On November 24, Theo joined his parents for their move into the new presbytery. A month later, the entire family was reunited, except for Anna, who had to remain in England.

Vincent's Fall, Theo's Rise

As soon as he returned to Paris, Vincent wrote Theo announcing he was quitting the Boussod Gallery. In actual fact, he had left work to join his family at Christmas without bothering to ask permission. His decision was no mere impulse as Vincent had already spoken about it with Theo and his parents. His manager had objected to Vincent's casual attitude, and after a stormy discussion, Vincent was obliged to resign. Theo was stunned.

Despite his disapproval of Vincent's behavior, Theo was a paragon of solidarity. He understood the weariness and desire to rebel that had prompted his brother's actions, and he was thrilled by Vincent's bravado. He himself would never have dared to take such risks—his temperament prevented him from taking chances": too many unfortunate consequences would result from his inability to take risks.

If Vincent was experiencing a setback, Theo, for his part, was winning his spurs at the gallery. His learning and his professionalism pleased his employers, who enthusiastically sent him on the annual sales trip; his task was to visit clients around the country and present the new catalog to them. In March 1876, he was traveling down the roads of Holland, meeting with the collectors and art lovers who patronized the gallery to show them the latest items. Dorus and Anna were delighted by his new assignment. Theo's father proudly wrote: "I find it a marvelous thing for you and hope that it will be successful."[37]

However, Dorus and Anna worried about Vincent, who had gone back to England, where he was teaching French, German, and mathematics in a shabby boarding school in Ramsgate in exchange for room and board. It was a difficult and wretched life.

Theo never faltered in his support for his brother, maybe because he wanted to compensate for the pride his parents felt for him and not for Vincent. It was clear that Theo was the family's glory, Vincent their disappointment.

In July, Vincent became a teacher and the assistant of a pastor, Slade Jones, in Isleworth, England. So consumed was he by his burning faith, that he was thinking of dedicating his life to bringing the Gospel to the poor. His halo was becoming tarnished in his parents' eyes. The van Goghs increasingly feared that the community would find out about their son's erratic behavior. At the same time, Theo and his success gave them more joy and made them prouder than ever.

His success, however, was interrupted by a serious illness in late September 1876. He was bedridden with a fever that kept him from working. A doctor examined him, prescribed doses of quinine and rest, and declared that he would soon be well. When Theo's uncle Jan, a retired vice admiral, heard of his condition, he visited the patient and informed Theo's mother. Immediately thereafter she wrote her son that now she understood why she had not heard from him. Miss Roos, who was there, looked after him, but his condition worsened. Roos and Tersteeg told Dorus van Gogh that even though the doctor's diagnosis gave no cause for fear, the fever persisted. The situation continued to be worrisome. Theo's parents wrote Theo nearly every day. Finally, almost a week after Theo became ill, they received a reassuring telegram from Theo's employer, and Jan also sent the good news, but noted that the fever, loss of appetite, and lack of sleep had left Theo seriously weak.

Dorus was alarmed by this; a few days later, he made the trip to The Hague. When he arrived, distraught, he found Theo in bed, dazed, and staring vacantly. Dorus sat at the foot of the bed, watching patiently and praying for his recovery. Theo's condition did not improve, and the family feared the worst. But at last, the crisis passed. A telegram was sent to inform Anna, who had been consumed with worry.

On October 19, Dorus was back in Etten, with Anna taking her turn with their son. Four days later, she returned to her husband at the presbytery: Theo was better, but not well enough to travel as far as Etten to rest.

In early November, Theo gathered the energy to make the trip, and began his convalescence at his parents' home, where he had a quiet, sunny little room at the back of the house. Dorus and Anna treated him like a king, anticipating his slightest whims—something a colleague who also boarded at the Rooses teased him about. As for Vincent, the gravity of his brother's illness had been kept from him.

Theo quickly regained his strength and soon missed being at work; when he mentioned this to Tersteeg, his employer advised him to continue getting better. Three weeks later, finally back on his feet, Theo returned to The Hague and his activities. His employer was very understanding, and all Theo's friends and acquaintances were models of loyalty and kindness. His illness demonstrated to Theo that he could count on others. His father adds: "This must be a reason to appreciate life all the more, and to enjoy it in good cheer with God's goodness."[38]

And yet, Theo seemed unable to enjoy anything. Nothing made him happy. His "easy life," as he called it, made no sense to him. Unlike artists, who were creative and struggled for their work, or his parents, who were imbued with a mission, Theo felt useless. Vincent writes: "There was a sentence in your letter that struck me, 'I wish I were far away from everything, I am the cause of all, and bring only sorrow to everybody, I alone have brought all this misery on myself and others.'"[39]

Clearly, Theo was suffering from a severe depression, an illness that ran in the family. His paternal grandfather and his uncles Cent and Hein were depressives. There turned out to be epileptics on his mother's side, including Anna's sister.

Dorus and Anna, frightened by this mental illness, stayed as close to their darling child as they could. Fortunately, Theo was saved by his love for his profession. He grabbed on to life again, just as Vincent—now living in Holland again and hoping to become a minister—was beginning to retreat from it.

Though Theo embraced his work, he could no longer stand The Hague. The city had too many painful memories. In 1877 Tersteeg again assigned him to the sales tour around Holland, and in 1878 his life took a new direction. His superiors gave him the honor of representing the gallery at the company's stand at the prestigious Paris World's Fair.

3 PARIS–THE HOPE OF SUCCESS

1878-1883

M AY 1, 1878. The excitement coursing through the French capital on the first day of the World's Fair contrasted with the gloom that had pervaded the country since the humiliating defeat by the Germans in 1870 and the tragic events of the Commune.

Paris was celebrating. The streets were decorated with French flags and teemed with a mass of people that hindered the circulation of the hackney cabs. There were the sounds of firecrackers exploding. Popular songs echoed on the boulevards. The wounds of war were a thing of the past. It was peacetime, and the burgeoning Third Republic wanted to spread that message across the city.

The mild weather had allowed the crowd to gather since dawn for the inauguration of the fair, at the doors of the

EDGAR DEGAS, *The Absinthe Drinker*, 1875–76.
Musée d'Orsay, Paris

Trocadéro, built on the Chaillot hill. This curious Hispano-Moorish-style construction with a central rotunda, was dominated by the reproduction of a sculpture by Antonin Mercié, *Fame*, whose head was wreathed with the garland of peace.[1] This building housed the galleries of art and culture, while, across the way, the Champ-de-Mars was dedicated to commerce and industry. Nearby, visitors could explore the inside of the monumental head of Frédéric-Auguste Bartholdi's statue of Liberty. (This gift from the people of France to the United States, marking the centenary of their independence, inspired some to quip that liberty has no brains.) But the fair's main attraction, in the courtyard of the Tuileries, was the *Grand Captif*, a tethered balloon with a volume of some 32,000 cubic yards and a diameter of 117 feet. This aerostat was higher than the Arc de Triomphe, and its gondola could carry 50 people an astonishing 1,625 feet into the air, by means of a steam-winch-operated cable. There were more than fifty thousand exhibitors and almost ten thousand foreign visitors from thirty-five countries—except, of course, Germany.[2] Paris, at the heart of the modern world, would blaze with a thousand lights until October 31.

In Paris, where the next phase of Theo's life was beginning, he celebrated his twenty-first birthday on the day of the inauguration of the fair. He was now a young man intent on tasting life's pleasures, yet because of his painful experiences in The Hague he had already lost the carefree quality a man of his age should have. He was a serious young man, much older than his years.

The first impressions were promising. Theo had formed his ideas of Paris from what his uncle Cent had told him and Vincent had written him; now, the fair gave him the opportunity to discover the French capital's wealth and cultural riches for himself. He marveled at Thomas Edison's phonograph, which was introduced at the fair; admired the magical lighting effects; and discovered the countries of the world in their pavilions on the Rue des Nations. The Japanese pavilion, in particular, was creating a sensation. During the Meiji period, the country was opening up to the West, which had a voracious appetite for anything made in the Japanese style, especially art and furniture. The clean lines of the lacquers, ivories, porcelains, and embroideries were all the more attractive compared to the overly ornamented Western objects. Intellectuals praised the freedom, refinement, and colors of Japanese prints, and the Impressionists, especially Edouard Manet, were very much inspired by them.

Theo was incredibly lucky. As the representative of the house of Goupil, it was his job to introduce paintings by the gallery's artists to connoisseurs and collectors. He was at the heart of *the* Paris event only briefly—for the duration of the fair—but the experience would determine the rest of his career.

The gallery's works epitomized the academicism of the "French Painting" section of the World's Fair, which was very conservative. The jury that had selected the paintings had deliberately ignored any of the more avant-garde work, such as that by Honoré Daumier; the paintings of peasants by Jean-François Millet, whose canvases the van Gogh brothers very much admired; or the works of Gustave Courbet, a very political artist and avowed Socialist. (Though it is true that one of Courbet's paintings was accepted, *The Wave* was unlikely to cause a stir with either the authorities or visitors.[3]) It is not surprising that the Impressionists were not represented, since their paintings were arousing great controversy in the art world and among the general public. The

French Third Republic was determined to deploy its cultural policy to emphasize the constructive, less controversial aspects of art created during the new regime. Because of this, the masters of academic art—an art familiar to and identified and appreciated by the hanging committee and the public—were over-represented.

Emile Zola, the prominent writer, was assigned to cover the fair for a Russian newspaper. In his review, his scorn for the work of academic painters that filled the fair was clear. He wrote: on Alexandre Cabanel, "always that same flabby draftsmanship, those same lackluster colors"; on Jean-Léon Gérôme, "mannered, . . . the same industriousness, like convicts carving coconuts"; and on Adolphe-William Bouguereau that his "painting is just as pompous."[4] He also lambasted Jean-Louis-Ernest Meissonier, a painter who had turned to battle scenes under Napoleon III and was the great success of the fair. Cabanel, Gérôme, and Meissonier, all members of the Institute, also received the Beaux-Arts medal of honor for painting. In sculpture, similar kinds of conservative work were featured. Even Auguste Rodin, despite being already well known, if not famous, was not represented.

Anna and Dorus were proud of Theo. His professional conscientiousness had finally caught his superiors' attention. "Many will envy you, and everyone who knows you think you deserve it, and we all agree that this appears to be very good for your future. It will certainly be a great opportunity to make yourself known. All our hearts go with you on this voyage and will follow you, and we pray for a blessing upon you."[5]

And yet the van Gogh parents, unfamiliar with the French capital, worried about Theo's Paris trip; in their eyes, their son was being exposed to every peril. They reminded their son to turn to his faith for support, though he had already distanced himself from religion. Anna also advised him to eat properly, take the time to sleep, and not to catch cold. They also encouraged him to make the most of this opportunity.

Theo was living in a boardinghouse on Rue de La-Tour-d'Auvergne, in a little garret room. It was a neighborhood of Paris that Vincent knew well. Every morning, Theo was awakened by the melodious song of the caged birds of a nearby tailor. For a brief instant, his mind would wander to the quiet of the Dutch countryside. But he had just enough time to get ready, stand on a chair—the only way he could see the view over Paris from the dormer window—and gaze at "thundery skies like the ones Bonington painted."[6] He had not a moment to lose; they were waiting for him at the booth. He had rapidly become indispensable: his employers liked his seriousness and his hardworking nature, but they were especially surprised by Theo's erudition and the ease with which he could explain the subtleties of painting.

An important encounter would also militate in his favor. The French president Patrice de Mac-Mahon, on an official visit to the French painting wing, stopped at the Goupil booth and asked Theo a few questions. All eyes were on this unknown man who was deep in conversation with the head of state. For a few seconds, Theo was suddenly at the center of the world.

It was a meeting that could have given the shy young man a nervous breakdown. But he rose to the occasion. Theo replied intelligently and with ease. This chance encounter revealed the young man to be an excellent addition to the Goupil gallery.

Outside of work, Theo was living a very full life. The Hammans, Protestant friends of the family, treated him like a son and invited him to dinner regularly. With another friend, Frans Braat, who worked at the gallery Boussod et Valadon, Theo walked the capital's brightly lit streets. To please Caroline Haanebeek-Van Stockum, he looked after Pieter Boele, a writer and bookseller and friend of hers, then in Paris.

At the end of August, Cent, his wife, and Theo's other uncle Cor, very intrigued by the fair and curious to see how their young nephew was getting along in the outside world, joined him in Paris. It was a chance to exchange news about everyone, and especially about the event that had the van Gogh family very excited: the marriage of Theo and Vincent's sister Anna.

Dorus and Anna's little house in Etten was vibrating with an unusual frenzy—with laughter, crying, and constant comings and goings. Everything had to be ready for the big day as it was the family's first marriage. Anna was marrying Joan van Houten, a serious young man whom Dorus and Anna trusted completely. Anna, who had been worn down by problems with her health, was gradually getting better. Everyone was there, even Vincent, who had returned home in July. When he quit, he had been preparing for the entrance exam for the Department of Theology in Amsterdam, and his parents had been greatly troubled. Fortunately, Pastor Jones of Islesworth, who was passing through Etten, suggested finding a Flemish preparatory school for evangelists in Brussels that would accept Vincent. The only shadow over their happiness was Theo's absence; professional obligations kept him in Paris. He had to be content with sending splendid reproductions as a wedding gift.

On August 22, 1878, under a sunny sky, the reverend was very moved as he witnessed his daughter's marriage in the small village church. Many from the community attended the ceremony, happy to congratulate the van Gogh family, which had reunited for the occasion. The young newlyweds were leaving Etten that evening to live in Leiden. There were affectionate farewells on the steps of the church, promises to see one another soon, and a few tears. Soon after, life returned to normal. Three days later, Vincent left for Brussels with Dorus and Pastor Jones.

Not everything in Paris was going well for Theo. It exasperated him to be confined to the Goupil booth all day long, repeating the same monotonous tasks. There was no possibility of his going to work in one of the Paris galleries, so he felt he was losing ground professionally. Even more disheartening was the fact that his performance at the fair was arousing the jealousy of the Paris employees, who made it clear that a foreigner should not have represented the company instead of them. Their animosity was troubling to him, and he wrote his father about it. The pastor both comforts and warns him: "Then keep up your guard, do not trust unconditionally every friendship offered you; think of intrigues! that are also ascribed to that metropolis! be a man twice warned!"[7] Theo also turned for advice to Cent, who after Vincent's defection had placed all his hopes in Theo and now urged his nephew to "show yourself and keep close to the Gentlemen [Boussod & Valadon]."[8] Easier said than done; Theo was incapable of placing himself in the best light and playing the game by joining the conversations of these prominent men. The only solution was to keep working hard, trust in his abilities, and make himself indispensable. This was how the van Goghs had made a place for themselves in society, and Theo began to see the merits of their philosophy.

He remained in Paris until the fair was over. Cent, then in Princenhage, congratulates him: "You were able to come through all these difficulties and reach the end of your engagement. It would have been disappointing and bothersome if you had left in the middle. I hope you have learned one thing in life: that everything is not rosy, and that every trade has its share of difficulties. And you will often laugh at the minor annoyances of your first stay in Paris."[9]

A Break with Vincent

ON NOVEMBER 15, 1878, on his way back to Holland, Theo stopped in Laeken, where Mastor Bokma's school, which prepared missionaries going to poor countries, had accepted Vincent. There, in that Brussels suburb, Vincent was already imagining himself converting whole populations. The reunion reawakened the feelings of their former intimacy. Excited by the prospect of a more radiant future, they walked alone, just the two of them, as they had in Zundert. At the museum, they both stopped before the canvases of Hendrik Leys and Charles Corneille Auguste de Groux. Vincent expressed their shared emotion: "How rich art is, if one can only remember what one has seen, one is never empty of thoughts or truly lonely, never alone."[10]

The magnificent weather and their happiness together, made it an unforgettable day. Theo gave Vincent two engravings and bought him an etching titled *The Three Mills*. After Theo left, Vincent felt the need to write him immediately. He added a small drawing, *In the Coalfields*, that he had sketched by a towpath. It showed a little tavern of the kind where workers go to eat their bread. It represented a level of poverty he was to know personally.

Soon after Vincent's enjoyable visit with his brother, he received disappointing news: he was deemed unsuited to be a preacher. Devastated, he left to teach the Bible in a mining region near the French border. In January 1879, he was granted permission to go preach for six months in Wasmes, in the Borinage, a desolate coal-mining area. After being exposed to the hard life of workers in the outskirts of London, he was now confronted with wretched conditions among the Belgians. He was overwhelmed by the experience: "Around the mine are poor miners' huts, a few dead trees black from smoke, thorn hedges, dunghills, ash dumps, heaps of useless coal, etc."[11] All around him were beggarly, ghostlike children and women doubled over beneath the weight of coal sacks.

Vincent had come to help these unfortunate men and women with his passionate preaching of his faith, but he saw that they needed far more than any religious guidance. Choosing the way of humility and poverty, he gave away what little he had, down to his clothing and linen. From now on, he wanted to live like them, share their harsh existence. He went so far as to go down the mine for six hours, into that dark, dangerous place when an accident could happen at any time. On April 16 an accident did occur: there was a pit-gas explosion in Frameries, a village near Wasmes. In a letter from Dorus to Theo, Dorus shares his concern: "It is very upsetting, that terrible accident, and now I read in the Courant that a strike will result, I hope that that will not now cause difficulties for Vincent . . . with all the eccentricities that he has, there still was real interest for those unfortunates."[12] It was precisely his zeal and commitment that irritated his superiors, and they did not extend his mission. Yet another setback. Undaunted, Vincent returned as a volunteer to the coal country, this time to Cuesmes. And so he continued to pursue his mission of charity in yet another town and live in extreme poverty; but the people of the Borinage would long remember their redheaded pastor, that odd, but very generous man dressed in sacking.

THE SITUATION WORRIED HIS PARENTS, who could not quite understand their eldest son. "Tomorrow it will be ten years since Vincent left our house, and I accompanied him to The Hague to work in the Goupil business. What sadness since that time! What pains, which we have felt day and night over him. We are tired and almost despondent—even though we remain firm in our faith and that he is a child in God's provenance."[13] At their wits' end, they turn to their son Theo for comfort, as usual: "And we again give you the assurance that we need you and that you are our crown and our joy."[14]

Since their time together in Laeken, Theo and Vincent were growing more distant. While Vincent was living in penury, Theo was climbing up the social ladder. In early 1879, in The Hague, he received a pay raise, and an extraordinary bonus, probably in recognition for his performance at the fair. His parents were proud of his good fortune. In April Tersteeg told him he would be sharing in the profits and promised he would soon be working in Paris. The pastor seemed surprised at the news, but congratulated his son: "We were surprised by the contents of your letter and of the plan that you talk of, to go back to Paris. Well, fellow! That is a great change! . . . How delightful for you, since it will give you a real position and what is more it will win the trust of these Gentlemen."[15]

At first the proposal delighted Theo, who had discussed his future career with Tersteeg. Yet neither the position nor the salary was what he had expected: he would be merely an assistant in one of the Paris branches, the one in Montmartre. Dorus, surprised, had questions: "You see disappointments . . . Can there be something hidden behind all this? You have talked to me of the manner of intrigues, and of some employees looking at you with green eyes . . . I s it possible to live in Paris for 150 francs per month . . . But it will now be doubly difficult because you were in better circumstances there [in Brussels] . . . do not give up hope . . . "[16]

Anna was in Paris herself, at Cent's sickbed; he was suffering greatly. She was surprised to discover how luxuriously her brother-in-law lived, a way of life she could not have imagined. When she told him of the offer that Theo had received, Cent, despite being very ill, discussed it with Boussod. Anna reported the conversation to her son: "Uncle was not very happy, but he said you will have to accept it. Mr. Boussod told you that you must start at the lowest and then climb up the scale."[17] The road to success was certainly paved with obstacles, but the Protestant education that his parents had inculcated in him had prepared Theo for the serious effort necessary to advance. He acceded to the consensus of opinion, and agreed to leave The Hague for Paris, despite the unsatisfactory terms, in the humble hopes of making a place for himself. His departure was planned for October 6, 1879. The final move would take place in November.

On August 14, 1879, before leaving The Hague, Theo visited Vincent, who was still in Cuesmes. They were writing each other less often; during this period everything seemed to exacerbate the contrast between their very different lives. One had goals, prospects for the future, and a desire to be an art dealer. The other, struggling in the world of the abjectly poor, felt his faith abandoning him and reality catching up with him; he escaped his pain by making small drawings.

As they walked, they realized they had become strangers to each other. Seeing Vincent so miserable, an exasperated Theo spoke for the family: "Pa, Moe, the uncles, and Anna don't understand why you can't yet support yourself. You, Vincent, the only one who was able to study." He reproached Vincent for behaving as if he were a man of independent means and to substantiate his admonishments counted off the trades he could have pursued. The list included such diverse professions as "an engraver of invoice headings and visiting cards, or a bookkeeper or a carpenter's apprentice," as Vincent writes, asking whether he should perhaps "follow the advice of my very dear sister Anna to devote myself to the baker's trade or many other similar things (curiously at odds and hardly compatible) that other people advise me. But you say, 'I do not expect you to take that advice literally; I was just afraid you were too fond of spending your days in idleness, and I thought you should put an end to it.'"[19] By the time Theo left his brother, Vincent was utterly at a loss. Their friendship and mutual confidence had completely vanished over the course of their time together. Their correspondence would be stilled for almost a year, from October 1879 until July 1880.

In Paris, Theo, the conscientious employee, was intent on proving his desire to be hired onto the gallery staff. Hoping his efforts would be noticed, he worked diligently and made progress.

Vincent's Turning Point

MEANWHILE, VINCENT WAS FIGHTING to give a direction to his life. The misery amid which he lived depressed him. Believing that he ought to live like the miners and share their distress he slept on the bare ground, ate the crusts of charity, and shared his bread with the elderly. It was in these wretched circumstances that Vincent, in July 1880, at twenty-seven years of age, felt a resurgence of energy. He wanted to follow a new course, to focus on the only goal that offered him any hope—his pleasure in painting. He decided, with Theo's support, to give his life a new aim, to devote that life to art, which held mystical associations for him. Just then, he learned that the money that his parents gave him came from Theo. He wrote his brother "reluctantly" to thank him. In that long, poignant letter, Vincent assessed his failures and mistakes; he tried to reestablish a connection, to restore the intimacy that had once been so cherished between them. "Do you know what makes the prison disappear? Every deep, genuine affection. Being friends, being brothers, loving, that is what opens the prison, with supreme power, by some magic force."[20]

This is a crucial document in Vincent's voluminous correspondence to Theo. It allows us to understand Vincent's development and how he came to make his decision, and it reveals the process that was necessary for such a change to take place. He would forge a new direction, this time in tandem with his brother. They would go down that road together, as he had long dreamed of doing. Moved by what he read, Theo made an important decision: he would take Vincent's career in hand. If his brother wanted to paint, Theo could give him much advice, share his thoughts on art, and give him both moral and material support. He began giving Vincent one hundred francs a month, which eventually became one hundred fifty (a sum made possible by Theo's rising salary) as painting materials, models, and food were expensive.

Theo would respect their agreement all his life. What underlies such a commitment? It was their shared passion for art, the symbolism of the vow they made at Rijswijk, Theo's affection for his brother, and his innate generosity.

Theo's Double Life

THEO CONTINUED TO RISE IN HIS PROFESSION. He was a model employee, putting his heart and soul into the gallery. Nevertheless, his parents still treated him, at twenty-three, as if he were still a child. Anna showered him with advice: "Before leaving for the gallery, make sure you eat properly, because the way you describe your life, you need to be master of your nerves to remain very, very strong."[21] Her solicitude was matched only by his pastor father's: "But always think on the rules on healthy living, good food at all times, proper sleep and keep an eye to Him who is the spring of all that is good. "[22]

ABOUT A YEAR AFTER RETURNING TO PARIS, Theo's efforts were rewarded: the gallery's owners assigned him a position of his own. In February 1881, as young as he was, he was named manager of the small Goupil gallery on Boulevard Montmartre. The entire family congratulated him warmly. For the occasion, Vincent wrote him a letter in French, as if in celebration of the event.

Theo now appeared to have a steady, comfortable situation: he was earning four thousand francs a year, or about three hundred francs a month.[23] It was a respectable—even, by some standards, enviable—salary. These numbers convey the significance of the amount that Theo took out every month for Vincent: exactly half, besides the help he gave other members of the family. If he was going to make ends meet, he had to be persuasive with the clients, since he also made a commission on the sales of paintings. In addition, over and above his salary, he received 7½ percent of the net profits made annually by the branch office.

At the same time, his position with the firm was not and never would be completely secure. His contract stipulated that Boussod and Valadon retained the absolute right to terminate their manager's position and send him away at any time, without any explanation or compensation.[24] Theo suffered from anxiety attacks as a result of this uneasy situation, and his employers' ingratitude would plague him for his entire life.

NEVERTHELESS, Theo's new financial condition allowed him to leave his room at Rue de La-Tour-d'Auvergne—where he had first lived during the World's Fair—to move not too far away, to Rue Laval—today Rue Victor Massé—into a proper apartment.

Theo lived and worked in the ninth arrondissement, which was at the time the vibrant heart of the city. It was the chic quarter, attracting every facet of fashionable Parisian society: the theatrical, literary, and artistic worlds converged here, as did the business world. An arrondissement with typical Haussmann architecture, where a very heterogeneous group of people met and mixed, it was a place full of energy, always intensely lively, where trends were created. It was where foreigners became *flâneurs*, and Parisians thronged. These masses strolled the streets and admired the latest fashions in the windows of the Printemps department store, frequented the many restaurants and cafés; or went to the theater or the Opéra Garnier, inaugurated in 1875. Nearby, on Rue Drouot, the Hôtel des Ventes—the auction house—

attracted art collectors and art lovers. A few steps away, galleries had opened. While Paul Durand-Ruel, Georges Petit, and the Bernheim-Jeunes championed the Impressionists and other much-criticized avant-garde artists, the well-known and prosperous firm of Goupil was still promoting "good taste" in art and continued to sell what was fashionable in art. Boussod and Valadon similarly took no risks—their artists, esteemed by bourgeois society, epitomized the moral order and profited from the endorsement of the Paris Salon. The Salon effectively tyrannized the arts, determining what artistic concepts would prevail, what the state would acquire, official commissions, and trends in the art market, as well as deciding the careers of painters. Without the blessing of the Salon, artists had little chance of success, making a name for themselves, or making a decent living from their painting.

Besides the gallery that Theo managed, Goupil had opened their flagship shop at Place de l'Opéra in 1872. It was a luxurious, stiffly proper environment, where wealthy collectors were lost in admiration in front of paintings enhanced by subtle lighting, and where academicism was favored: from pompous history scenes, to military subjects and polished pink nudes, such as the allegorical nudes from Alexandre Cabanel and Adolphe-William Bouguereau, and Neoclassical nudes from Jean-Léon Gérôme, the leader of this highly regarded classicism. Gérôme, decorated with the Legion of Honor, was Alexandre Goupil's son-in-law and Etienne Boussod's father-in-law. He was also one of the most admired painters of the latter half of the nineteenth century; his paintings sold for astronomical sums, and he shed his unique luster on the house of Goupil. Their contract with him granting them exclusive reproduction rights earned the gallery enormous profits. His prestige was international, since young painters from around the world boasted of studying with him at the Ecole des Beaux-Arts. All his work reflects the conventions of official art: the hierarchy of genres; the primacy of drawing; the systematic study of drapery and the nude; the rejection of *plein air* painting; a glossy finish and invisible brushstrokes; and constant references to antiquity and the Italian Renaissance.

Fiercely antagonistic to the new movement in art, Gérôme raged against the Impressionists. The 1884 Manet retrospective, some of the paintings in which had influenced the work of Gérôme's students, aroused Gérôme's fury: "There's the result of the garbage that some schemers have wanted to expose you to!"[25] Impressionism had been making headlines since 1874, the year of its first exhibition, held at the gallery of the photographer Nadar. Camille Pissarro, Paul Cézanne, Edgar Degas, Pierre-Auguste Renoir, Alfred Sisley, Armand Guillaumin, Berthe Morisot, and Claude Monet—all well-known now—were not yet names to be reckoned with. At the time, the general public hated their paintings, considering them "poorly finished" and contrary to the traditional cult of beauty. The subjects of the avant-garde painters were the moments of daily life, and this went against the prevailing taste, which deemed them too prosaic to be celebrated in high art.

We do not know whether Theo had the opportunity, when he ran into the gallery's star painter, to discuss with Gérôme the radical changes taking place in the artistic milieu and the developments in painting. Had this occurred, the conversation between the two would certainly have been contentious, since their positions on the topic were clearly diametrically opposed. Theo was soon enthralled by this "new manner" of painting, as it was known, where the emphasis was on the spontaneity in creating a painting, a spontaneity that was seen to have given way to a sense of liberation, even emancipation. The beauty of those luminous, light-colored, and vibrant paintings that captured the ephemeral effects of light fascinated him. He felt respect and profound admiration for those talented painters who were revolutionizing the art world. Their spirit of rebellion against the prevailing rigidity and the struggle they waged against the staid finish and exceptional orderliness of official painting struck a chord in the young dealer. He understood that a great change in the art world was on the horizon. Theo identified the various avant-garde currents, and then gradually began to explore how he might promote these innovations.

His attraction first to the Realists, then to the Impressionists, and later to the Post-Impressionists was unlikely to endear him to either Boussod or Valadon, and their differences of opinion aggravated their complex relationship. Theo, of course, had to accede to the firm's direction, but he deplored his employers' narrow mindedness, and their conventional and conservative taste. Seeking relief from the tense atmosphere that sometimes permeated the company, Theo felt the need for renewal and to get far from that environment. In 1881 he joined the Dutch Club so he could meet his compatriots. It was a place to talk about the old country, have a drink, and play billiards. This was where Theo would meet Andries Bonger from Amsterdam, who would become his closest friend.

Andries, known as Dries, was born in 1861 and came to Paris in 1879 to work with a broker, Geo Whery. His salary was low, and he slept in a folding counter at the office, because it was larger than the place where he lived. He was very religious, and attended the church on avenue de la Grande-Armée every Sunday, to hear Pastor Bertier's sermons. Serious and solitary by nature, Dries did not suffer gladly his fellow Dutchmen's somewhat boorish and bawdy manners: "But I would make an exception for M. van Gogh, the son of a pastor. He is very clever when talking about art. It is because of him I am staying in the club." [26] Both young men were interested in literature, though their tastes differed. For Theo, Zola was to literature what Degas was to painting—the undisputed master. Despite their differences, their love of art, a desire to learn and to improve themselves, and their loneliness in Paris brought them closer together. Every Sunday, they met to look at the masterpieces in the Louvre, discussed developments in the world of painting, and compared points of view. Theo, who always expatiated on his artistic discoveries to Dries, was much bolder in his preferences than his friend.

They also bonded through their love of nature, going for long walks in the woods. Theo's longing for his native countryside never diminished: "I love the tranquility of the countryside & the fatigue one feels after being out in the fresh air is quite splendid."[27]

The two men were both finding it difficult to adjust to the French capital. Theo, who would never really adapt to life in Paris, often felt ill at ease there. The behavior of the French confused and embarrassed him. He had been raised in a family where it was normal to be honest, to be straightforward with others, to trust them, and to establish sincere relationships. Theo deplored the superficiality of the people among whom he found himself: "The more people one meets, the more one sees that they hide behind conventional forms of conversation, and that what they say when they pretend to be honest, is often so empty and so false. Bonger, who is a good friend, is different, and we often say to each other that although we meet many people, we meet so few people whom we find sympathetic."[28] He complained regularly about the Parisians' lack of warmth and their indifference. His letters reveal both his homesickness and melancholy: "I am surrounded by people for whom I have lots of sympathy. And yet there is nothing that appears like a more intimate relationship, as exists in Holland. One meets people in the street, in the restaurant, in cafés, sometimes in their houses, but even then one has the feeling of being in a waiting room from which one is soon going to leave. You don't see anything in life as we can see it at home. One cannot make out if So-and-so is happy or unhappy with his wife. . . . "[29]

This may be why Theo—who had to maintain a distinguished appearance at the gallery, and was always correctly dressed in a three-piece suit in order to please the bourgeois clientele—was drawn to the bohemian life, the night life. The artists' impertinent but free manners bewitched him. Theo liberated himself from Goupil's strict and uptight world by regular visits to Montmartre, a quarter of modest dwellings taken over by poets and Impressionist painters. This area of Paris came to symbolize the Parisian bohemians, and Montmartre became famous—or notorious—through their verses, songs, stories, and paintings. Artists liked meeting there because the neighborhood retained its villagelike character and rebellious spirit. Among the lower classes, far from the conventions dictated by the bourgeoisie, they could live as they pleased, be themselves. At the Moulin de la Galette, an outdoor café set up around an old windmill—which Renoir famously painted in 1876—men and women danced to accordion music.

La Nouvelle-Athènes became the artists' favorite place. Café Guerbois, which until 1875 had been the Impressionists' hangout, had been abandoned, the Thursday gatherings now only a memory; it was superseded by the brasserie on Place Pigalle, the perfect spot for the enthusiasm of these effervescent men. This café was famous as a rendezvous for dissidents during the reign of Napoleon III, and the avant-garde found this appropriate: were not they, too, resistants, fighting the power of the Salon? Renoir and Degas, who lived not too far away, were regulars, and it was at La Nouvelle-Athènes that Degas painted *The Absinthe Drinker* (pg. 56), which represented friends of his—the colorful engraver and painter Marcellin Desboutin and one of the Impressionists' favorite models, Ellen Andrée—seated at a table, one with an innocent beverage, the other with the nearly toxic drink of the title. Manet, Jean-François Raffaëlli, Pissarro, Paul Gauguin, and Gustave Caillebotte, as well as Monet, when he was in Paris, joined Renoir and Degas. It was not unusual to encounter literati there, too, people such as Philippe Burty, a great patron of the Impressionists, or Edmond Duranty, founder of the magazine *Réalisme* and author of the important book *La Nouvelle Peinture: À propos du groupe d'artistes qui expose dans les galeries Durand-Ruel.* And, of course, there was Zola. Everyone, including the waiters, engaged in heated discussions about art, with the Impressionists, Neo-Impressionists, and Divisionists all arguing for their respective camps. Pissarro brought his Neo-Impressionist friends to this establishment. Georges Seurat and Paul Signac were there, alongside Gauguin and Guillaumin, with whom they heartily disagreed, and Henri de Toulouse-Lautrec. The whole crew stormed the nightclubs, which were awash in the green wave of absinthe, a drink so strong and so unhealthy that it made people insane.

This was how the nightclubs became fashionable, and made the quarter famous. The most popular places were the Cabaret des Assassins—which would become the Lapin Agile—the Mirliton, where the poet and singer-songwriter Aristide Bruant burlesqued the clientele, and the Chat Noir. The Picard painter Rodolphe Salis intended his establishment to be a literary cabaret, where talent, impudence, and provocation would embody the Montmartre spirit. He had opened the Chat Noir in 1881 in his studio on Boulevard Rochechouart; the name came from the title of a painting he had been commissioned to make from a story by Edgar Allan Poe. When, in 1885, the Chat Noir became too successful for its small site, it transferred to Rue Laval, very near where Theo lived, making it all the easier to frequent.

Once through the club's door—which was defended by a Swiss Guard armed with a halberd—a visitor might be surprised by the haphazardly decorated space. Emile Goudeau describes it as follows: "A cat in a gibbet; another cat in the stained-glass window; wooden tables; big, square, massive chairs; enormous Passion nails; tapestries hanging all along the walls, above diamond-shaped panels torn from old chests."[30] Completing the décor were a fireplace adorned with a warming pan and a skull (Louis XIII's, the joke went) and a monumental counter nearly collapsing beneath the weight of bottles and glasses. On the walls were drawings and engravings by Marcellin Desboutin, Jean-Francois Raffaëlli, Adolphe Willette, and Jean-Louis Forain. The waiters, dressed in green like members of the Académie, addressed customers as "prince" or "monseigneur." The back room was reserved for the regulars, who had the privilege of rubbing elbows with politicians and literary luminaries such as Zola. Poets like Paul Verlaine, Alphonse Allais, Maurice Donnay, and

Emile Goudeau, and draftsmen such as Albert Robida exercised their talents for the greater pleasure of a clientele of habitués made up at first of artists and anarchists, but also of those marginalized by society—panderers and prostitutes.

In this debauched setting, Theo was a familiar face, with his own table, at which it was not unusual to see Henri Rivière, a penniless young artist who had created a shadow theater.

Theo was entirely at ease in this exciting, licentious world, where he felt accepted. His nights, unlike his days, were happy. Although he was neither extroverted nor eccentric, Theo was nonetheless curiously in tune with Salis, the loud-mouthed owner. The bohemian world was a realm of limitless fantasy, and in it Theo tasted the happiness of a freedom that was nowhere to be found in his professional environment. In Montmartre, no one judged him. There, he could express the feelings and emotions that he repressed or suppressed in his daily life. He and the regulars talked as equals—class distinctions played no part in those relationships. In Montmartre, Theo, without any inhibitions, enjoyed the pleasures of life in Paris. In short, Theo was alive there.

One night, during one of his customary strolls in the quarter, he met a woman who was alone and in distress and who touched him.

Rescuing a Lost Soul

THERE ARE AMPLE DETAILS about Vincent's chaotic love life; they include his disappointment with Eugenie in London and his exalted love in 1881 for Kee Voss— a young cousin—a widow and the mother of a small boy in Etten for the holidays. But for the same period, there is little information on Theo's romantic relationships. Nothing emerges from his letters to his parents or sisters, and discretion on the subject was de rigueur in the van Gogh family. In the best of cases, Theo felt awkward enough talking about his private life with his intimates, let alone when it was about more delicate matters.

In January 1883, Vincent refers in his writings to a woman with the first name Marie. Evidently disturbed by this young woman, Theo felt the need to unburden himself to his older brother. He was baffled by the relationship. His serious, reflective nature was stymied by his powerful feelings. Vincent reassured him: ". . . [W]hen I think it over, I am relatively confident of the result. Such a feeling is not 'passion,' for a deep, fathomless pity is at the root of it. Nor do I believe that such a thing makes you unfit for thinking about other things; on the contrary, it has a serious character which rouses and strengthens all your faculties and augments rather than diminishes your energy."[31]

If Theo hoped to get answers from Vincent, it was because Vincent had been living since 1882 with Sien, a prostitute he had met in the streets of The Hague, a woman whose fallen state had instantly touched his charitable heart. Their affair continued, against the family's collective advice and in spite of the resulting scandal.

Vincent and Sien. Theo and Marie. Two parallel stories of forbidden and complicated love, a shared experience that brought the two brothers even closer together. "Generally speaking (apart from the difference between the two persons in question), to you and me there appeared on the cold, cruel pavement a sad, pitiful woman's figure, and neither you nor I passed it by—we both stopped and followed the human impulse of our hearts."[32]

Theo's Breton mistress, whose last name remains unknown, had suffered a wretched existence. ". . . [S]he has known other things beside poverty and narrow-mindedness. . . ." Vincent writes.[33] These "other things" to which Vincent prudishly refers certainly mean prostitution. The letters reveal that she had paid the debts of the man she had lived with previously, by performing sexual favors.[34] At this time, it was not unusual for a woman of very modest means to have to prostitute herself occasionally. Even women whose husbands had lost their jobs often found themselves walking the streets of Paris.

Touched by Marie's misfortunes, Theo wanted to take her away from her lurid life. Vincent advises him: "It would be desirable for her to be elsewhere than in a dreary hotel room—she ought to have more homelike surroundings. . . . [T]he sooner she returns to ordinary everyday activities and surroundings, the better."[35]

The relationship created problems for Theo. For four years, during the daytime he had been moving in very bourgeois circles, quite different from the world he inhabited by night. This worried him and Vincent as well: "It would be better to be circumspect where the firm is concerned, because they could ruin everything. . . . How will they interpret things? Will the matter cause a conflict with the firm?"[36] Would Theo be obliged always to keep his affair a secret? Other questions gnawed at him, too: Was Marie a woman for him? Would she make him happy? Vincent believed Marie would be faithful and forever grateful to the man who made it possible for her to forget the events of her unfortunate past. Vincent was convinced that Marie was perfect for Theo— more convinced than Theo.

Finally, around April, Theo made up his mind to

reveal to his family the existence of the woman who was sharing his life. He hoped to marry Marie in five months. The van Goghs did not receive the news well. Dorus and Anna had not the slightest idea of what had been going on in Paris. Now they were suddenly discovering not only that there was a woman in their son's life, but that there would be a wedding. They registered their disapproval in no uncertain terms. Dorus wrote to his son and told him the situation was completely unacceptable and told Theo to give up his hopes of marrying her.

Vincent, siding with Theo, reacted violently to their parents' stand. Revealing their disapproval of his own similar situation, he writes to Theo: "But, Theo, now that in your case—knowing that you have a permanent position and a good salary (nota bene, considerably more than their own)—they raise the same objection, I can only say that I think it unutterably pretentious and downright ungodly."[37] But Theo did eventually end the relationship, through it continued (according to Vincent's correspondence) until 1884. However difficult the breakup was, the relationship could not withstand the seemingly endless obstacles to its continuation.

The Support of the Family

In gaining his independence in Paris, Theo took upon himself the crushing role of the family's support, replacing his parents as he made the important decisions—especially those concerning Vincent.

Dorus and Anna, powerless before and baffled by their eldest son's strange behavior, had long ago given up trying to influence him. Because Theo had been supporting Vincent financially since Vincent had dedicated himself to painting, it fell to Theo to take care of everything, especially finding solutions to the vicissitudes of his life. Theo was Vincent's only ally in his struggle to take charge of his destiny. From Paris, where he belonged to a brilliant cultural world, Theo wrote his brother, then isolated in Holland, about his impressions and discoveries. He helped Vincent as best he could, by sending him reproductions of works by many artists, including Millet—for Vincent, the ultimate master. When his older brother was taking courses in Brussels at the Académie des Beaux-Arts, Theo told him to look up Anton Van Rappard, a young Dutch painter. Despite the difference in their social classes—Van Rappard was the son of a wealthy family—Theo hoped that the two would be able to share their knowledge of painting. The encounter went well, and Van Rappard would remain a faithful friend of Vincent until 1885, when they argued about *The Potato Eaters* (fig. 1), the painting that would prove to be the most important work of Vincent's Dutch period.

A RELATIONSHIP AS INTENSE as the one between Vincent and Theo could not always go smoothly. Vincent was difficult; his rages, incessant reproaches, and tirades would have irritated the most easygoing temperaments. The diplomatic Theo tolerated most of Vincent's excesses, except when Vincent lashed out at his mother and father. When this occurred, Theo immediately put Vincent in his place. This happened, for example, after Vincent left Etten for The Hague: "I think it is a very good thing that you have settled permanently in The Hague and hope to do as much as I can to help you out until you can start earning your own money. But what I do not approve of is

FIG. 1: VINCENT VAN GOGH, *The Potato Eaters*, 1885.
Van Gogh Museum, Amsterdam

the way in which you contrived to leave Father and Mother, That you could not bear it there is possible and that you should differ in your views from people who have lived in the country all their lives and who have had no chance of participating in modern life, is only too natural, but what the devil made you so childish and so shameless as to embitter Father and Father's life and render it almost impossible by setting about things in the way you did? . . . Is it not a bitter pill for Father to swallow to see himself belittled by someone who claims to be more of a freethinker, and whom, au fond [deep down], he possibly envies from time to time for his clearer insights? Does his life count for nothing then? I don't understand you."[38]

Despite his incomprehension, despite their arguments, despite everything, Theo looked after Vincent. His commitment implied responsibilities, as he was well aware, and he accepted them. The question of money was always at the heart of their relationship. It was vital if Vincent was to pursue his work, and this constant preoccupation was a source of anxiety for Theo. Every month he had to pay out the amount he had promised his brother in 1880. His family also counted on him. The pastor had never earned a proper living; now, in Neunen, at the end of his career, he was making eleven hundred florins a year. Theo helped him out by regularly defraying his parents' expenses, and it was thanks to Theo's help that Cor, the youngest brother, was able to train as a metallurgical apprentice.

The constant concern about money plagued Theo the rest of his life. The gallery was in serious difficulties in late 1883, when Vincent was painting in Drenthe, a marshy region in northern Holland with a very harsh climate (fig. 2). Vincent was on his own there, after ending his relationship with Sien, a decision taken under pressure from Theo, who mediated between his parents and his brother to calm everyone down.

This time, it was Theo who was desperately troubled: among other reasons, the August 1883 sales were disappointing. There were also differences of opinion between his employers and himself concerning the direction the business should take. Theo wanted to open the gallery to new markets, but the directors of the house of Goupil refused. They went around and around with the same arguments, more or less acrimoniously. Now, at year's end, the situation seemed hopeless and untenable. Theo could no longer tolerate being considered a minor employee, with no real power.

FIG. 2: VINCENT VAN GOGH, *Plowman with a Horse and Two Women*, sketch from letter from Vincent to Theo, dated October 13, 1883.

During such sensitive periods, the depressive side of his nature came to the fore, and he would be racked by negative thoughts, torn between the desire to let everything go and the need to go on in order to support the family.

Knowing his brother well, and given to the same inner contradictions, Vincent soothed Theo by reminding him that he was not alone. As was his way, Vincent was overzealous in defending Theo's position, which gave Vincent the opportunity to disparage Goupil, who symbolized to him the profiteers making money on the artists' backs. He advised Theo not to be docile, but to react forcefully against the humiliations piled on him by the firm's directors. He writes: "It is too much to bear alone, and in part, at least, I can sympathize with you. Now, stick to your point, and don't let your grief let you lose your head; if the gentlemen behave like that, then stand on your honor, and do not accept your dismissal except on conditions which guarantee your getting a new situation."[39] This was exactly the opposite of Dorus and Anna's advice: "Take the time if you have troubles. . . . Arm yourself against difficulties and be wise and courageous."[40]

In fact, Theo was growing tired of being biddable and judicious. In the gallery, watching the ceaseless traffic of passersby on the boulevard, he dreamed of going away. New York beckoned: with a public more open to the avant-garde, it might promise a new beginning. He could open his own gallery, finally be taken seriously. Theo told his uncles of his plans, and meanwhile continued studying English.

The possibility of Theo leaving was a frightening prospect for Vincent. Even though he was encouraging his brother to leave Goupil and work for another dealer, he could not face the possibility that Theo might move so far away. Without Theo, without those powerful roots and that strong connection, how could he survive? In an effort to convince Theo to stay, Vincent exhorted him to become a painter himself. It was an idea he had advanced in The Hague, but without insisting. In this letter, Vincent quotes from an earlier letter to his brother: "'. . . I do not know whether you are really a man of business; actually I see the artist in you at heart, the true artist. . . .'"[41] He continues later in the letter: "I cannot help imagining the future, when I should no longer be alone, but you and I, painters, working together as comrades here in this moorland."[42]

Vincent manically constructed career plans for the two of them, calculating how much money they would need to live in Drenthe, that inhospitable region. Vincent imagined the wild beauty of that desolate landscape would, in its own way, provide inspiration. Art would be their only sustenance—it was a noble dream.

Vincent offered another possibility: which was to return to the comfort of his family: "In case Theo considers it advisable that my expenses be reduced to a minimum and I should have to live at home for a while, I hope, for myself as much as for you, that we shall possess the wisdom not to make a mess of things by discord, and that, ignoring the past, we shall resign ourselves to what the new circumstances may bring."[43] It was unclear whether the entire family would be prepared to make sacrifices for the sake of Theo's happiness.

The solutions that Vincent suggested verged on utopian. Did they conceal selfish ulterior motives, or a lack of any sense of reality? Why would Theo consider one of the most unstable of careers—a painter—when he had worked so hard to advance in that of art dealer? Besides which, he loved his profession, and had no desire to change it. Theo, gnawed by indecision, was in torment. His generous, altruistic nature curbed his reactions. He did decide eventually, and with some relief, to remain in his position with Goupil; to forget, albeit regretfully, his dream of America; to come to terms with Boussod and Valadon's dictates; and to remember that it was advisable to be humble and courageous. He elected to follow the code of the van Goghs: "You are a man with a will, and a good, intelligent, clear head, with an honest heart."[44] Such was Theo's nature. His concern for others would always take precedence before his own aspirations.

Vincent van Gogh, *Open Bible, Extinguished Candle, and a Novel*, 1885. Van Gogh Museum, Amsterdam

4 BREAKTHROUGHS
1884-1888

FACED WITH HIS BROTHER'S REFUSAL to join him in Drenthe, Vincent finally made up his mind to stay for a time in Neunen, where his father had been pastor since 1882. At the time, the village's population was about twenty-five hundred, many of them Catholic and most of them weavers or farmers. It was the humblest of all of Dorus's parishes.

No sooner had he moved in with his parents, than Vincent clashed with his father, directing his anger at the symbol of so-called Christian morality. Their relationship very quickly deteriorated, and the family environment became fraught. Vincent directed his anger not only at Dorus—Theo, too, was included in his critique of society. Theo, responsible for all of Vincent's misfortunes in Vincent's eyes, became his favorite target, the object of his rages, his scapegoat.

Every letter to his brother during this difficult period contained an avalanche of reproaches, and before long Theo had had enough. Dorus advised him to remain calm: "You will surely receive a letter from Vincent, but above all don't quarrel with him too much. He is not well and feels feverish. I wanted to ask you to remain calm. He is very irritated and irritable."[1] But how could Theo maintain his equanimity when he was unfairly subjected to Vincent's vitriole, a brother for whom he had done so much? Theo reached the limits of his patience and understanding.

Vincent blamed his brother for his breakup with Sien. Out of bravado, he declared that he intended to live with her again. His brother's reply was direct—he asked Vincent how he planned to support Sien with no money. Instead of keeping silent, Vincent instead became even more enraged. The exchanges escalated: since Theo disapproved of Vincent's choices and his way of life, there was no point in continuing their relationship: "I do not want to get embroiled in a second series of quarrels, of the kind I had with Father I, with Father II—Father II being yourself. One is enough."[2]

It seems clear from the correspondence that what Vincent yearned for was Theo's approval and appreciation of his art. "I really do know exactly why we yoked ourselves to the task as friends, respecting each other. I know that I wouldn't be able to let it degenerate into protection.—Theo, I don't want to become your protégé. . . . You do absolutely nothing to provide me with a little entertainment, when I sometimes need it so badly—by establishing friendships for me or giving me enough money to have fun from time to time. . . . You can't give me a wife, you can't give me a child, you can't get me work. But money, *that* you can give me. What good is it if I have to do without everything else? Your money remains sterile. . . ."[3] At this point in their relationship, the correspondence between the two brothers, with its bitterness and drama, begins to sound like a romantic relationship.

Vincent broached with his brother the delicate subject of selling his paintings, accusing Theo of making no effort to market them. Despite this lack of commercial interest, Vincent persevered, and his paintings and watercolors developed and became more mature. He considered himself a witness to the dreadful conditions of the peasants, miners, and weavers in the areas where he had lived. And these were the people who filled his paintings.

By now, Vincent ranked Theo among his enemies—that is, art dealers. Vincent despised them because he believed they made money on the backs of artists, who struggled to create their art. In Vincent's eyes, Theo had joined the bourgeoisie. His morality and way of life had changed; his well-cut clothes and carefully trimmed moustache were representative of this new phase in his life.

During 1884 and 1885, a very clear abyss opened between them, though Anna's accident—a fracture of the femur—brought about a truce. The brothers were both distressed at their mother's suffering; Vincent, the one at home, took it upon himself to make her life easier by lavishing her with attention. His devotion touched Theo as well as Anna herself.

The suspension of hostilities was short-lived; Vincent very soon returned to his diatribes against Theo, with even greater conviction. His tone became more and more aggressive. The painter wrote that he increasingly wanted to make his living from his work. He despised his brother as he did the Goupil directors: "I dread certain things that are bound to occur—namely that people will say, how strange, don't you do any business with your brother or with Goupil? Well, what I'll say then, is—'it is beneath the dignity of Ces Messieurs G. & Co., Van Gogh & Co.'"[4]

Theo was unable to take the risk of exhibiting work that was not only by an amateur but by his own brother in such a conservative gallery. Because Theo socialized in avant-garde circles, he was well aware of the difficult struggle that certain painters faced in an effort to be recognized. He had been interested for some years in exhibiting work by the Impressionists, Monet and Degas, for example, who were just beginning to attract an audience of faithful collectors. By dint of perseverance, in 1884 he was finally able to sell a landscape by Camille Pissarro to the art enthusiast Guyotin for 150 francs.[5] The following year, he was able to sell three paintings—one by Sisley, a *Jardin* (Garden) by Renoir, and a landscape by Monet—to Victor Desfossés, an important Paris collector.[6] The return was certainly not huge, but Theo was encouraged. Little by little, he was achieving his goal of selling the paintings that moved him. Boussod and Valadon tolerated Theo engaging in these transactions because he did quite well for them in 1884. This was an extraordinary feat, given the profound recession France had been experiencing for a decade or so, and in 1884 in particular it had been very severe. Theo imparted the excellent news to his parents, who rushed to congratulate him.[7]

THEO WAS CERTAINLY AN ASSET TO THE GALLERY. In time, his abilities came to be well known in Paris, so much so, that he received an offer from one of the gallery's competitors. Theo refused, perhaps because he thought the situation with his employers was improving.[8] Exasperated by his brother's letters, he responded to Vincent's barrage of insults with silence. As he grew angrier, however, he reacted to Vincent's rage with brutal honesty: he found Vincent's work rather unoriginal. Sensitive as Theo was to the Impressionists' process and to the luminosity emanating from their canvases, he seemed to find no value—at least no commercial value—in his brother's efforts. Vincent responds to Theo's assessment of his work: "Conclusion: You indicate that if my drawings were so beautiful that you could put them next to Millet's and Daumier's, you would occupy yourself with them."[9]

Vincent, though angry and hurt, never failed to demand his monthly allowance in every letter. During this period of crisis, Theo sent Vincent more money than usual, about two hundred francs, so that Vincent might buy the materials he needed and settle the debts he had accumulated in The Hague. This financial imperative prevented the painter from making a final break with his brother.

It was at this time that Vincent proposed a sort of pact to his brother: in exchange for his monthly allowance, Theo would own all of Vincent's work. It was, it seemed, the only solution left for a desperate man who would not, at any price, cut the ties with the brother who supported him: "Of course I will send you my work every month. As you say, that work will be your property then, and I perfectly agree with you that you have every right to do anything with it; even I couldn't make any objection if you should want to tear it to pieces. . . . I must have money, in order to get on; I try to get it, and therefore— even if you were completely indifferent to me—as long as I get your monthly allowance, without conditions forbidding me to do certain things, I will not break with you, and I agree to everything if need be."[10] He closes with a stinging remark:

"My way of considering you and your money matches your way of considering me and my work."

Their agreement was inconvenient for Theo. Becoming Vincent's dealer meant becoming even more embroiled in their pact. And yet, being sensitive and kind, he knew very well that his promise to his brother entailed obligations. If he accepted Vincent's proposal, it was out of brotherly love, but also out of a desire for peace. During this time, he discerned no particular talent in Vincent's work, no doubt because the work had not yet matured. Theo was now an experienced dealer who knew the art market very well and could immediately identify the canvases that would find buyers. He also knew that Vincent was working desperately hard to produce "acceptable" paintings, and that he was putting all his energy, rage, and creative powers into his work. Theo also knew Vincent had to paint to survive. For all these reasons, Theo had to honor his promise to his brother. From that time, in exchange for 150 francs a month, he agreed to receive Vincent's works, to own them, even have the right to destroy them. At this point, Theo was not only in a paternal role, but was taking on the responsibilities very much like that of a foster mother, as Viviane Forrester suggests.[11] Vincent and Theo were now inextricably linked.

The Pastor's Death

AN UNFORESEEABLE EVENT brought these two brothers together. On March 26, 1885, in the first days of spring, their father returned from a long walk, suffered an attack, and collapsed at the door of the presbytery. He died suddenly, at only sixty-three years of age. The day before he died, he had written Theo a letter full of graciousness, in which he thanked his son "for always thinking of us and making our life sweeter by his attention and his comforting words."[12]

This sudden turn of events stunned the entire family, including Vincent, despite his ongoing conflict with Dorus. Adding to Vincent's distress was the fact that the funeral took place on Vincent's thirty-second birthday.

On March 30, 1885, Pastor Theodorus van Gogh was buried in the Neunen cemetery, near an old abandoned tower that today no longer exists. Besides the immediate family, members of the church, and people from the village, many from the area wished to pay their last respects to the dedicated reverend. The many flowers evidenced the affection and esteem people felt for him. He was remembered by the open grave with great emotion. The speakers praised the pastor's courage, piety, love of others, and mercifulness. Dorus was a fixture of the Brabant countryside, and those in attendance thought of the figure of that good man walking miles in rain or wind to preach.

The many speeches touched Anna deeply, but they could not soothe her anguish. The man she had so cherished was gone. The entire family stayed with her to support her during this time: uncles Cent and Cor; Pastor Stricker; her sisters; and her children, including Anna and her husband, and Theo, who had left Paris immediately upon hearing of Dorus's death. In the family's common sorrow, the grief-stricken young art dealer became close to them once again.

Curiously, Theo and Vincent's correspondence after the burial reveals no particular sorrow, whereas other sources attest to the distress they shared. Andries Bonger told his parents that on April 4 he had seen Theo, "who was still greatly saddened by his father's death,"[13] while Vincent executed a still life in the pastor's memory. Next to a vase of flowers—intended to be symbolic, because in English they are called "honesty"—he drew his father's pipe and tobacco pouch. In another painting, *Still Life with Bible* (pg. 90), which demonstrates more explicitly the complexity of Vincent's relations with Dorus, a candle and an imposing Bible are contrasted with Emile Zola's novel *How Jolly Life Is*. Vincent's very ambivalent behavior toward the pastor was rooted in his extraordinary admiration for him. Since childhood, Vincent had placed his father on a pedestal, and when he had considered a career as a preacher, his pastor father was his ideal. As time went on, however, their differences of opinion and quarrels about the church poisoned their relationship, and a distance grew between them. Above all, Vincent had never forgiven him for attempting to have him committed to an asylum after his failure in the Borinage, as he considered Vincent too eccentric, almost insane.

Theo's case was entirely different. The younger son loved his father very much, but did not idolize him. He understood the pastor was a fervent believer who meant to live by the precepts of Christian morality. All his life, he practiced these principles, raising his children lovingly and strictly. Living far from the many temptations of the cosmopolitan world, he sought neither money nor accolades, but he could be narrow-minded and intolerant. Theo had been able to forgive him, and accept all the different facets of the father he respected.

With Dorus's death, Theo was now officially the head of the family, the sole support of his mother, and his siblings— Wil, Cor, and, of course, Vincent. Everyone counted on him, and the situation worried him. Although he made a respectable living, it was, after all, the commissions he earned on the sales of paintings that provided a modicum of financial comfort. "Father's death has caused you many extra expenses," Vincent acknowledged.[14] When Cor, the youngest brother, went to work and brought in his first earnings, we can feel Theo's immense relief. Happy to congratulate him, Theo immediately writes: "I heard this morning from Wil that tomorrow, for the first time, you will receive a salary. I cannot let the day go by without telling you that I want to wish you much happiness. You have proven that you have energy. . . . You can earn your bread by your own powers. . . . So keep up the good work, my lad, and be careful, stand on your own two feet. Being dependent is very limiting, both of oneself and for others. If you continue to be a good worker, you will find your path."[15] Theo's words eerily resemble those of Dorus and Anna when he began working and making a living. When Theo mentions dependence and its negative effects, he was of course, alluding to Vincent.

The pastor's death contributed to Theo and Vincent's reconciliation. Vincent seemed glad and relieved to see his brother again, share his sorrow, and talk about art. Grief had erased the rancor between the two men. When Theo came to Neunen for their father's burial, Vincent dragged his brother into the vast studio he was renting from Schafrath, the Catholic sexton, to show him his latest works, in particular sketches for the painting *The Potato Eaters*, a work that would become famous. The dark, very realistic canvas portrays the life of the peasants of Brabant, their faces marked by their grueling toil. Theo, ever sensitive, was immediately touched by the painting's power. It was the first sign of approval of his work that Vincent had so been hoping for.

Upon his return to Paris, Theo began showing Vincent's work to a select few, and was pleased to be able to report to his brother, and to the family, that his canvases had met with an encouraging reception: "I was glad to give Vincent some good news. The man who gave me his opinion on his paintings is someone who has experience and an infallible judgment. I haven't sold anything, but that will come. . . . How I hope that his work will bear fruit."[16] Theo had taken a few canvases, including *The Potato Eaters*, to Alphonse Portier, a draper turned paint-shop owner, who was in contact with the Impressionist painters Pissarro, Monet, and Degas, among others. "Several people have seen his work, either at my house or at Portier's, and find it very promising. Some have found his painting beautiful, because it is true and authentic, and faithfully depicts the peasants' and weavers' misery."[17]

Nevertheless, Theo remained cautious. Because he saw the difficulties faced daily even by painters who were somewhat known, he knew Vincent's path would not be easy. The fact that Vincent's paintings were being seen by artists and connoisseurs was already a first step. Although Theo did not yet recognize his brother's talent, he felt an ineffable power emanating from his work. A letter from Theo to his sister Elisabeth (Lies) sums up his impressions of Vincent and his painting: "You ask me about Vincent. He is one of those people who has seen the world from nearby and has retreated from it. We shall now have to wait and see whether he has genius. I do believe it, and a few others with me, amongst them Bonger. Once his work becomes good he will become a great man."[18]

The pastor's death, which allowed Theo and Vincent to reconcile, caused a break between Vincent and his family. When it came time to discuss the pastor's estate, arguments broke out and resentments surfaced. The sisters, especially Anna, held that Vincent had no right to his share of the inheritance: as the eldest, their brother had had the advantage of a formal education, and at thirty-two years old he was still being supported, thanks to the family's—and especially Theo's—sacrifices. In order not to aggravate the situation, and confronted with so much pettiness, Vincent renounced his meager portion.

The family's animosity and the still-vivid memory of the failed suicide of Margot Begemann (a woman from Neunen who had become infatuated with him) prompted him to leave for Antwerp in November 1885 to pursue his career. He enrolled in the Académie des Beaux-Arts in January 1886, but soon found the school's narrow-mindedness and teachings, as well as the negative comments of the other students, intolerable. He was desperately lonely. Barely eating, he was wasting away from one day to the next, depriving himself of food to pay for brushes and paints. With this regimen of deprivation, he soon fell ill, complaining of dizziness and terrible stomach pains. Vincent wanted to leave the city that had rejected him. An idea took shape: he would go to the only person who understood him—his brother Theo.

A Burdensome Arrangement

FOR SOME WEEKS, Vincent had been writing Theo about his desire to go to Paris. Theo was reluctant to give in to Vincent's demands, and did not answer or was evasive, so as not to bruise his brother's brittle feelings. Then he advised Vincent to wait until July.

Since Vincent could not afford lodging, Theo would have to take him in, and he had serious misgivings about living with Vincent, whose behavior was erratic, swinging between joyful exuberance and ornery intolerance. The two brothers were extremely close, but sharing everyday life could be problematic indeed.

Confronted with Theo's silence, Vincent decided to surprise him: sometime around March 1, Theo, who was at the gallery, received a note from Vincent announcing his arrival that same morning: "Don't be angry with me for arriving out of the blue. I've given it so much thought and I'm sure we'll gain time this way. Shall be at the Louvre from midday onwards, or earlier if you like. Please let me know what time you can get to the Salle Carrée. As far as expenses are concerned, I repeat that it won't make much difference. I still have some money left, of course, and I want to talk to you before spending any of it. We'll sort everything out, you'll see."[19] The artist, clearly determined, made the first move without worrying about what his younger brother might think—he intended to pursue his work in Paris no matter what.

At first, Vincent was dazed by Paris's ebullience, and indeed the capital was experiencing a particularly fertile cultural moment. The artistic climate was rich with innovative tendencies, and all the painters knew and influenced one another in the splendid osmosis that characterized this period. In 1886, four large exhibitions displayed different aspects of the art being produced at the time. In May, the official Salon would be held, and, there, Albert Besnard's paintings would attract a bourgeois public. Concurrently, the eighth (and last) Impressionist exhibition would open in June. It marked the birth of Post-Impressionism, replacing an Impressionism that seemed to have exhausted its vitality. Georges Seurat showed his painting *Sunday Afternoon on the Island of La Grande Jatte*, which would become the manifesto of Pointillism, a pictorial expression that employs the objective laws of optics to replace the emotional subjectivity of vision. His aesthetic was shared by Paul Signac, Camille Pissarro, and Camille's son, Lucien. Degas exhibited a series of pastels. Only Guillaumin, Berthe Morisot, and Gauguin were showing Impressionist paintings. At that time, Renoir and Monet—whose works were beginning to increase in value—were represented in the fifth International Exhibition, organized at Georges Petit's gallery, Durand-Ruel's chief competitor. Finally, in August, the Salon des Indépendants would be held at the Tuileries, where Seurat would show his celebrated painting.

Vincent was overwhelmed. When he went into the gallery that Theo managed, he didn't know where to look first—there was so much art to see. The walls were covered with paintings by Corot, Daumier, the Barbizon School, and the Symbolist Gustave Moreau; in a discreet corner were a few Impressionist canvases. He was transported by his enthusiasm for everything he saw. Because Theo had entrée to all the exhibitions in the city, Vincent happily discovered the various currents in the painting of the period, but was also disoriented by the profusion of ideas being explored. Because he had spent years creating art isolated from other artists, producing his work in solitary conditions, it was difficult for him to imagine, despite Theo's descriptions, the different trends and the many subtleties of the art he saw. Encouraged and inspired, he frenziedly began making new drawings. He enrolled in the Atelier Cormon, where he improved his draftsmanship by drawing from the nude and from plaster casts.

Vincent rediscovered Paris, appreciating for the first time the riches of the city he had earlier ignored, since during his first stay he had closed himself up in his room with only a Bible for company. Life in Paris was gratifying: he made friends in artistic circles, and created a social life for

Fig 1: Vincent van Gogh, *View from Vincent's Room on the Rue Lepic*, 1887. Van Gogh Museum, Amsterdam

Fig. 2: *The entry of Vincent and Theo's apartment building on Rue Lepic as it looks today.*

himself, while he enthusiastically went to work on his art,
exploring new pictorial solutions.

Not so with his brother. Because Theo's house was
now too small for the both of them, they decided to move to a
larger and more expensive apartment, in Montmartre, on
Rue Lepic, where the dealer Arsène Portier lived, and where
the Atelier Cormon had been located for a time (fig. 1 and 2).
The apartment, on the fourth floor, had a magnificent and
unusual view over Montmartre. The lower part of the street,
with the local market and many shops, was lively, in contrast
with the more peaceful upper section, which opened onto the

Butte. Lying beyond the building's porte cochere, with its sandstone-paved entryway, the courtyard opened into a large garden redolent with lilac and roses. Andries Bonger describes their living situation to his parents: "They have a large, spacious apartment and do their own housekeeping. They have taken an accomplished cook."[20]

Their home consisted of a kitchen and four rooms, the largest of which was Vincent's studio. It was an eclectic space, decorated with engravings after Millet and drawing and paintings; among these, *The Potato Eaters* held pride of place. Vincent was comfortable there. The apartment also allowed Theo to receive his favorite painters and his friends in attractive surroundings. Chief among these friends was Andries, with whom Theo became very close when his father died. The trip to Holland they took in August 1885 strengthened their friendship, and gave them the opportunity to meet each other's families. On that fortuitous occasion, Theo was introduced to Andries's youngest sister, Johanna. Theo, instantly charmed, developed an immediate fondness for her. But as quickly as his feelings developed, he was informed that Johanna was in love with another man.

Back at Rue Lepic, despite the brothers' efforts to live together on good terms, their relations became strained. "Theo's brother is here for good, he is staying for at least three years to take a course of painting at Cormon's studio. If I am not mistaken, I mentioned to you last summer what a strange life his brother was leading. He has no manners whatsoever. He is at loggerheads with everyone. It really is a heavy burden for Theo to bear,"[21] reports Andries. Two months later he adds that "his brother is making life rather a burden to him, and reproaches him with all kinds of things of which he is quite innocent."[22]

Whatever the disagreements were, Theo made no mention of them in his letters to his family. On the contrary, he tries to emphasize Vincent's good qualities and the progress he is making with his painting. "Fortunately we're doing well in our new apartment. You would not recognize Vincent, he has changed so much, and it strikes other people even more than it does me. He has undergone an important operation in his mouth, for he had lost almost all his teeth through the bad condition of his stomach. The doctor says that he has now quite recovered. . . . He is progressing tremendously in his work and this is proved by the fact that he is becoming successful. He has not yet sold paintings for money, but is exchanging his work for other pictures. . . . There is a picture dealer who has now taken four of his paintings and has promised to arrange for an exhibition of his work next year. He is mainly painting flowers. . . . He is also more cheerful than in the past and people here like him. To give you proof: hardly a day passes that he is not asked to go to the studios of well-known painters, or they come to see him."[23]

Despite their problems, they persevered together. They frequented the brasseries on the boulevards, the beer gardens, and the cafés in Montmartre. At midday and in the evening, they met at Mother Bataille's restaurant in Rue des Abbesses. In this cramped, unpretentious, but very fashionable place, artists, cabaret singers, and writers crossed paths with prominent politicians—it was not unusual to see Jean Jaurès or François Coppée there. During the day, Theo was busy with his work at the gallery, while Vincent painted flowers, views of Paris, and windmills. Having quickly abandoned Cormon's teachings, he explored the area, visited the Paris museums, and went to exhibitions. Curiously, though he complained of not having enough money to pay models, and therefore had to paint still lifes, it did not occur to him to ask his brother to pose for him. It is an interesting fact to consider, given how much Vincent depended on his brother for nearly everything he did in his life. But in this, he did not rely on his brother, and instead turned again and again to his own visage, self-portraits that would become some of his most important works. Vincent's dependence on his brother would, however, cause the painter's behavior to become increasingly erratic.

Theo's yearly summer trip to Holland allowed him to gain some distance from Vincent. A new woman made an appearance in his life at this time. It was a very discreet affair, even her first name remains a mystery; she is designated merely by the initial S. Some biographers have suggested that she may have been Agostina Segatori, a former model for Corot and Gérôme who became the proprietor of the tavern Le Tambourin and is believed to have been Vincent's mistress for a time. This is now known to be incorrect: we know that Theo was involved with someone when Vincent arrived in Paris. In fact, this was one of the reasons he did not want his brother to live with him. A letter from Vincent, dating from 1886 and sent to Theo in Holland, clarifies the situation: Theo wished to discontinue the problematic relationship with his mistress because he still had strong feelings for Jo Bonger.[24] Living in Paris so far away from her had not diminished his powerful feelings.

In order to help his brother leave his mistress, Vincent came up with a foolish plan: he himself would take her as his companion, because he feared that a break would drive her to suicide or insanity. He claimed to be prepared to marry her, if a marriage of convenience could save her. In Theo's absence, Andries witnessed a strange psychodrama play itself out between Vincent and Theo's mistress, the woman identified in the letters only as S. Dries, who was more realistic than Vincent, advised against the marriage solution, but acknowledged that nothing should be done precipitately. Theo must have broken up with her, though the exact events are unknown. What is clear is that S never appears in his life again.

Theo also made the trip to Holland to ask the uncles if they would be willing to underwrite his plan to open an art gallery, where both brothers could devote themselves to the artists who interested them. Unfortunately, Theo was unable to convince them. His uncles were reluctant to see him associated with the clearly unstable Vincent, and were very surprised that Theo sought to promote painters who, in their eyes, were worthless. In their view, Theo would never get rich, as they had, by supporting such artists.

His dream of going out on his own was not yet possible; Theo was still bound to his employers. In the end, his only victory was to have convinced his family that Vincent had talent. "What a satisfaction for you, because of the firm confidence you have always had in him!" exclaims Andries in the note he included with Vincent's letter.

Upon returning to Paris on August 26, Theo found Vincent the same as always, vacillating between buoyant enthusiasm and ornery malcontentedness. Life went on, until, in December, Theo fell gravely ill. Andries reports in a letter to his parents: "Theo has had some serious problems with his nerves, to the point that he could no longer move. To my great surprise, yesterday I found him as before; he still felt a little stiff, as if after a fall, but otherwise he had no ill effects, now he will take better care of his health."[25] Theo's constitution was weak, and he would often be ill over the course of his life. He saw doctors regularly, one of whom

Andries introduced him to. Yet, despite all the medications Theo took, the pain continued to plague him unabated. He confides terrible things to Lies: "Now I can tell you that last winter I thought I would never celebrate my thirtieth birthday. No one knows, and it's better that way, because it would worry the family. Keep it to yourself. Now, everything has passed, and I am in better health than I have ever been. . . ."[26]

Unlike Theo, Vincent seemed to have inherited a sturdier constitution: he survived cold, hunger, and syphilis. In Paris, he consulted the same doctors as his brother, but received different treatments. This period of his life in Paris enabled him to regain a certain equilibrium, because he could eat as much as he pleased; he was now making the most of life.

BEGINNING IN 1887, Vincent socialized with the new generation of artists. At the Atelier Cormon, he had met Louis Anquetin, the vitriolic Toulouse-Lautrec, and the Australian painter John Russell who would execute a portrait of Vincent. Vincent met Guillaumin through Portier, and Theo put Vincent in touch with the former Communard and anarchist Julien Tanguy.[27] Affectionately nicknamed "Pere" by the artists, the color merchant enthusiastically supported avant-garde painting, believing these misunderstood artists to be geniuses who would soon achieve great success. He generously opened his doors to them, and in the spirit of a great patron of the arts, gave them unlimited credit to buy paints and canvases. His little shop on Rue Clauzel, not far from the church of Notre-Dame-de-Lorette, became the gathering place for artists rejected from the Salon and their friends.

Tanguy grew fond of the passionate Vincent and knew he was a great painter. In Tanguy's erstwhile meeting place of the avant-garde, Vincent became friends with Emile Bernard and met Paul Signac. He went often, to admire the works of Cézanne—another one who left paintings with Tanguy to sell. Taking a cue from other artists, Vincent was now painting *en plein air* at Asnières or Clichy with Signac. With Toulouse-Lautrec, he went to the Montmartre cabarets, including Le Mirliton, where the powerful singer Aristide Bruant performed. He attended the weekly artists' meetings that the painter of the Moulin-Rouge performers organized at his studio in Rue Caulaincourt. "He arrived, carrying a heavy canvas which he stood in a corner where it got a good light and then waited for some attention to be shown. But no one bothered. He sat opposite his picture, scrutinizing the others' glances, taking little part in the conversation, and finally he left wearied, taking his last work with him," Suzanne Valadon recalls.[28] Theo introduced him to the painter Camille Pissarro, who would prove a sincere and exceptional friend to both brothers, and later to Gauguin, whom Theo met at the home of the artist Claude-Emile Schuffenecker. After Gauguin returned from Martinique in late 1887, Vincent and Theo spent a great deal of time with him. Vincent, impressed by his height and the quality of his work, was soon a heartfelt admirer. And indeed, Gauguin was surprisingly voluble, self-assured, and determined to pursue his career as a painter, despite years of suffering and deprivation. He and Vincent spent their evenings talking together, with Gauguin reminiscing about his various travels, and Vincent envying his adventures. Vincent also acquired a taste for absinthe, which gave him nightmares and left him mentally unstable.

At the gallery where Theo worked, Vincent became familiar with the paintings of those he called the "painters of the *grand Boulevard*"—because they exhibited on those broad avenues—such as Monet, Degas, and Renoir. Vincent dreamed of creating a community of artists and founding a group of "painters of the *petit Boulevard*," that is the boulevard de Clichy, which would attract a clientele sensitive enough to be interested in the group's work. Gauguin, Bernard, Seurat, Signac, Anquetin, and Toulouse-Lautrec belonged to the group. A very motivated Vincent organized two exhibitions: one at the very popular restaurant Le Chalet, and the other at Le Tambourin, owned by his mistress, Agostina Segatori. Unfortunately, both were failures.

Nevertheless, Vincent was beginning to be a presence in the small circle of avant-garde artists. He exchanged canvases with certain painters—driving Theo to despair, since he had not yet sold a single work: "He has painted a few portraits which have turned out well, but he always does them for no payment. It is a pity that he does not seem to want to earn something, for if he did he could make some money here; well, you can't change a person."[29] Vincent's trades allowed Theo to form a collection, with paintings by Gauguin, Toulouse-Lautrec, and Bernard. At the same time, both brothers were wild about Japanese art, and purchased prints from Samuel Bing's, the Paris specialist in that art.

Vincent did not seem discouraged: he elected to dedicate himself to creating and perfecting his technique, rather than putting his energy toward selling his art. His painting gradually became more luminous and vivid. And it seemed his social skills were improving: despite his difficult personality, he behaved as if he were affable.

His freedom and bohemian life were in contrast with his brother's prosaic existence. Theo had to spend long hours at the gallery, put up with his employers' criticism, and earn money to support the family. His austere life during the day was confining. He did experience a free existence to some degree during his nighttime sorties in Montmartre, through his relationships with artists, and because of Vincent's daily presence, but it was impossible for him to give himself over to such a life.

At home, Vincent's behavior became increasingly difficult to tolerate. He was less able to tolerate the presence of his invasive, headstrong, and overbearing brother. At night, under the influence of alcohol, Vincent often launched into excited diatribes about art, during which he would insult his brother. He returned obsessively to the subject of the need to do something to support artists and exhorted his dealer brother to take up the fight. Faced with Vincent's relentless harangues, Theo felt helpless and despairing; at those moments, he was overcome by melancholy. He had no idea how to escape this impasse. The endless arguments with Vincent were making his life impossible.

He felt the need to confide in his sister Wil: "I am often ungrateful enough to imagine that I stand all alone and then the difficulties seem insurmountable and it seems there is no way out. If he was someone who had a different kind of job, I would certainly have done what you advised me a long time ago, and I have often asked myself whether it was not wrong always to help him; I have often been on the verge of letting him muddle along by himself. After getting your letter I again seriously thought about it and I feel that in the circumstances I cannot do anything but continue. It is certain that he is an artist and what he makes now may sometimes not be beautiful, but it will surely be of use to him later and then it may possibly be sublime, and it would be a shame if one kept him from his regular studies. . . . You should not think that it is the money side that worries me the most. It is mostly the idea that we sympathize so little anymore. There was a time when I loved Vincent a lot and he was my best friend but that is over now. It seems to be even worse from his side, for he never loses an opportunity to show me that he despises me and that I revolt him. That makes the situation at home almost unbearable. Nobody wants to come and see me, for that always leads to reproaches and he is also so dirty and untidy. . . . All I hope is that he will go and live by himself, and he has talked about this for a long time, but if I told him to leave that would only give him a reason to stay on. . . . It appears as if there are two different beings in him, the one marvelously gifted, fine and delicate, and the other selfish and heartless. . . . It is a pity he is his own enemy, for he makes life difficult not only for others but also for himself." [30] Theo resolved to go on as he had been doing.

A devoted Theo hoped to reestablish the peace—and he succeeded. A month later, Theo tells Wil of the truce: "We have made peace, for it did not do anybody any good to continue in that way, I hope it will last. . . . It would have been strange for me to live alone again and he would not have gained anything either. I asked him to stay. That will seem strange after all I wrote you recently, but it is no weakness on my side and as I feel much stronger than this winter, I am confident that I will be able to create an improvement in our relationship. We have drifted apart enough that it would not serve any purpose to make the rift any larger." [31]

The two men were now moving ahead together, working hand in glove. Theo admired Vincent, and Vincent believed in Theo. "Vincent is working hard as always and keeps progressing. His paintings are becoming lighter and he is trying very hard to put more sunlight into them. He is a curious chap, but what a head he has got, most enviable." [32]

They became aware that if their extraordinary relationship—which they both valued—were to last, they had better establish a certain distance between them. Vincent
understood that if he were to remain in Paris, Theo and he
would end up falling into their old, combative ways. Besides,
at this point he had had enough of frenetic Paris. He felt drawn
by the colors of the Midi, like Cézanne and Adolphe-Joseph-
Thomas Monticelli. The van Gogh brothers loved the lyricism
of the late Monticelli's paintings, so much so that Theo purchased a few for his personal collection. Vincent also hoped to
find landscapes like the ones in Japanese prints.

Vincent's Departure

In February 1888, Theo accompanied his brother to
the train station. He was going to Arles, in the south
of France. The night before he left, the brothers had gone to
hear a concert of Wagner's music. Music was an art form that
Theo was slowly coming to know and appreciate—he used
poetic metaphors to speak of it, as if it were visual represen-
tation. Before leaving Paris, Vincent asked his friend Emile
Bernard to help him arrange his canvases in the studio he was
leaving: Japanese crepons on the walls and a few of his luminous paintings on easels. He left the studio as he had kept it
over the years, intending to keep himself present in his
brother's mind. Their two years of sharing a home, an
important period in both their lives, had brought them much
closer—it was at this time Theo came into his own as a dealer
and Vincent's work developed more than it had previously.
Despite their many squabbles, they had found each other
once more, and a genuine intimacy had developed between
them. From this point on, their relationship was strong and

undisturbed by the issues that had separated them earlier. Vincent, persuaded that Theo was fighting to have his work and that of the Impressionists recognized, no longer considered him as an exploiter. For his part, Theo no longer doubted the talent and creative power that drove Vincent. Now inseparable, the two brothers would at last be able to shape the common project the painter dreamed of. Theo was more than just an art dealer—to Vincent, he was an artist, too.

Theo, feeling alone, almost abandoned, suffered from Vincent's absence. "When he came here two years ago I had not expected that we would become so much attached to each other, for now that I am alone in the apartment there is a decided emptiness about me. If I can find someone I will take him in, but it is not easy to replace someone like Vincent. It is unbelievable how much he knows and what a sane view he has of the world. . . . I am certain that he will make a name for himself. . . . In addition he has such a big heart that he always tries to do something for others. It's a pity for those who cannot understand him. . . . "[33] The connection between them had become vital to their equilibrium and existence.

While Vincent was settling in Arles and beginning his first paintings there, Theo languished. He was delighted to host his sister Wil for two days, and together they enjoyed the cultural riches that Paris offered. Theo was proud to introduce her to the painters he knew, and especially to "the master," Degas, who received them graciously in his studio. Wil's brief visit did not entirely quell Theo's sadness, and so, to keep his loneliness at bay, he hosted foreign artists on several occasions. The first of these, who stayed with him from February to June 1888, was the Dutch painter and friend of Vincent Arnold Hendrik Koning. The Danish painter Mourier Petersen followed Koning at Theo's Rue Lepic apartment.

Late that year, two Dutch painters bearing a letter of introduction for Theo appeared at the Goupil Gallery. Jacob de Haan, the son of an industrialist, surrendered management of his father's company to his brothers in exchange for an annuity that would allow him to devote himself to painting. Joseph Jacob Isaäcson was a friend. Theo invited them to stay with him, and it was in Theo's apartment that Meijer de Haan painted *View of Paris Taken from Theo van Gogh's Window on Rue Lepic*. Theo urged de Haan to study the Impressionists, and even sent Vincent some of the young man's studies. Through Theo, de Haan met Pissarro and Gauguin, whom he would join in Pont-Aven in 1889. Isaäcson was taking classes at the Ecole des Beaux-Arts and would become close to Bernard.

In a letter to Wil, Theo shares his discriminating critical opinion of the artists he is living with: "Meijer de Haan is a great painter, very attracted to avant-garde art. He is a little taken aback when he looks at Impressionist paintings, because he thinks his works from before are no good. His earlier works look something like Vincent's in Neunen, but without the fury. I find a hint of Rembrandt in his canvases. Otherwise, he has painted some splendid things since coming to Paris."[34] Theo was less moved by the work of Isaäcson, who had to paint family portraits to support himself, but both men were intelligent artists, whose company Theo enjoyed.

In Arles Vincent was frantically executing the first of his luminous works, and Theo was giving increasing attention to the painters he admired. His goal was to sell their work, but also to realize his and Vincent's ambition of supporting the artists of the avant-garde.

Dealer and Patron

"Theo is doing his best for all the impressionists; he has done something, or sold something, for every one of them, and he will certainly go on doing so. But the few things I wrote you about this question will show you that he is quite different from the other dealers, who do not care the least bit about the painters," Vincent writes Wil from Arles.[35] Theo must have been experiencing great satisfaction in Paris. Finally, his determination and persistence were bearing fruit. His strategy of wearing down Boussod and Valadon's resistance was paying off. In addition, a confluence of circumstances was accelerating the momentum: the problems faced by the Impressionists' main dealer, Paul Durand-Ruel. After fighting for the movement for some fifteen years, this enlightened art dealer was now going through a difficult period, because the collectors were reluctant to invest further in this style of painting. The exhibitions he had organized in London, Berlin, and Rotterdam in 1885 had not done very well. In 1886, however, when, at the invitation of the dealer James F. Sutton, he went to New York to show the works of the artists of his Paris gallery, they were well received. The following year, he exhibited in the United States again. In France his artists were feeling somewhat neglected: their dealer was no longer on the spot to look after their interests. They turned to other galleries that they hoped would be responsive. In 1887, for example, Monet, Renoir, Pissarro, and Sisley participated in the sixth International Exhibition at Georges Petit's gallery. At the same time, they approached the rather timid young Dutchman who was so interested in their artistic production.

Another change was taking place as well. In 1886 the

founder of the firm of Adolphe Goupil finally retired. Léon Boussod's sons Etienne and Jean took over the management of Boussod Valadon et Cie, which had been established in 1884. Theo hoped they would be open to a certain shift in direction. Because of Vincent's stay in Paris, the connections he had established with the new generation of painters—the "painters of the petit Boulevard"—made Theo's task easier. Now Theo was not only in contact with Monet, Degas, Camille Pissarro, Sisley, and Guillaumin, but also with Seurat, Bernard, Signac, Lucien Pissarro, Anquetin, and Toulouse-Lautrec. Theo, aware of Vincent's contribution, writes him in gratitude: "You may do something for me if you like—that is, go on as in the past, and create an entourage of artists and friends for us, something which I am absolutely incapable of doing by my own self."[36]

The Goupil gallery's ledgers indicate that in 1886 Theo purchased only one painting by Manet, who had died in 1883. He paid one hundred francs for it, and sold it for twice that to a painter, Frank Myers Boggs.[37] Theo, like Georges Petit, beginning in 1887, was encroaching on Durand-Ruel's dominance in the field. Theo was building a network of innovative painters and daring collectors. His precious address book contained contact information for prominent figures in the Parisian artistic sphere. Despite his very modest inroads into this aspect of the market, his employers agreed to devote the gallery's mezzanine to exhibitions of Impressionist, Post-Impressionist, and Pointillist works, as long as Theo continued to keep the gallery's profits high—as Theo had been doing easily ever since he had arrived. The ground floor would remain reserved for those artists who were sanctioned by the firm, and their paintings would be featured in the shop window that looked out onto the boulevard.

The mezzanine became an exhibition space where artists, collectors, and writers met to admire the works that were the talk of the town. The Symbolist poet Gustave Kahn describes the young gallery manager in his memoirs: "Theo van Gogh was pale, blond, and so melancholy that he seemed to carry canvases as beggars hold their wooden bowls. He expressed his beliefs about the worth of the art unenergetically, and thus ineffectively. He had no gift at all for sales patter. But that dealer was an excellent critic, and thanks to his love for and knowledge about art, he engaged in discussions with painters and writers."[38] It was a somewhat harsh assessment, though it was certainly true that Theo had neither the glibness of a slick salesman nor a knack for business. Yet the gallery's ledgers show that he made very good sales during his years with Goupil. He had the mind of a scholar who was more comfortable thinking about art than selling it, and his impeccable knowledge of art history earned him the respect of his colleagues and peers.

In May 1887, Monet writes Durand-Ruel, then in the United States, to tell him about the public's response to his paintings: "We are more popular with the buying public, no question. What will convey the idea better to you than anything I could say is that Boussod now carries some Degases and some Monets, and that it will carry some Sisleys and Renoirs as well."[39] Monet tended to embellish, however. Theo had started negotiating only with Monet and Sisley, not yet with Degas. As for Renoir, Theo never dealt directly with him. What is remarkable is that he had managed to establish a solid relationship with Monet. He went to Giverny regularly to admire the artist's new canvases. The brilliant orange-red of his sunsets and the trees' intense blue-green were compelling to him. Over the course of the year 1887, Theo bought fourteen paintings from him, for a total of about twenty thousand francs.[40] These paintings would all be sold to American collectors.

The prices of works by the increasingly popular Monet were beginning to rise. This was not the case with Pissarro's work, whose Pointillist canvases left Durand-Ruel, his dealer, unmoved. His paintings went for next to nothing, but Theo was able to sell two that Pissarro had left at the gallery on consignment for one thousand francs. After Boussod's commission, very little was left for the artist. Theo, who very much liked Pissarro's work, would always be vexed to see that the artist wasn't financially successful. "I sell almost nothing of what seems fine to me. Even the fan hasn't sold. When will we emerge from this period of indifference; it's certainly not the artists' fault."[41] For his part, Pissarro found Theo very generous, interesting, and intuitive: "I think Theo van Gogh, who is very astute, will be able to give me good advice."[42]

Despite the problems, Theo was encouraged by these small victories, and he took on other painters. He bought a canvas by Degas, *A Woman Seated beside a Vase of Flowers*, which according to the gallery's books sold for four thousand francs. The painter maintained regular but merely courteous relations with Theo. Theo was disappointed by this—he would have liked them to have been closer. The artist's laconic letters concern only the sales of his works. At this time, Theo was also marketing paintings by Sisley and Guillaumin, and sold a canvas by Gauguin for four hundred fifty francs to his most faithful collector, Dupuis, a wealthy industrialist. The penniless Gauguin was delighted; he wrote his wife that the Boussod and Valadon gallery had become the "center of the Impressionists."

And yet, almost imperceptibly, Theo was reaching his goal. Vincent rapturously urged him to keep going, in the hopes that Theo would finally be able to open his own gallery.

That would mean he could materially assist the painters by paying them a monthly stipend in exchange for their works. After much thought, and given Theo's uncles' refusal to contribute financially to his opening a gallery, the ever-prudent Theo decided not to leave his position. He did not want to take such a risk, preferring to keep his seven-thousand-franc-a-year salary and use it to support as best he could the artists he was championing.[43]

Theo continued to acquire paintings, from either the artists themselves or their agents or other dealers, or at the Drouot auction house. He also kept certain paintings on consignment, in case of a possible buyer. He tried to help those he could, such as Pissarro, to whom he sometimes advanced money. Reluctantly, the painter at times, had to ask his dealer and friend for financial assistance: "I shall be in financial difficulties around the first of October: rent, bills. . . . I'll need at least a thousand francs. I would be very grateful if you could see your way to helping me out. As soon as I'll have finished something, I'll send it to you."[44]

With his limited means, Theo filled in his personal collection by buying paintings he liked by little-known artists. He also began to organize group exhibitions. In January 1888, he showed canvases by Pissarro, Degas, Guillaumin, and Gauguin. For the first time, an enlightened public took the trouble to go see Gauguin's richly colored Martinique landscapes. Unfortunately, the show's reception was lukewarm. The art critic Félix Fénéon, in *La Revue Indépendante*, expressed reservations about the paintings and their startling technique. From a financial point of view, the exhibition was a failure—only Dupuis, a collector, bought a few paintings. This rich industrialist, who, believing himself ruined, would later commit suicide, acquired at least seventeen Impressionist paintings from Theo between 1887 and 1890. Theo was also able to sell six paintings by Gauguin in 1888, and would exhibit canvases by him again in November, including *Breton Girl Dancing*, which he sold in 1889.

Despite the lack of results from his first exhibition, Theo did not give up. Between March and October, he organized three exhibitions of Pissarro's work and showed lithographs by William Thornley and works by Rodin and Schuffenecker. In June of that year, he signed a contract with Monet. Monet had been annoyed at the attitude of his dealer, Durand-Ruel, who Monet believed was not supporting him as before. The artist very plainly reminded the dealer of his failure: "You say it is regrettable that I have accepted this commitment, but my dear M. Durand [sic], what would have become of me these last four years had it not been, first, for M. Petit, and without the house of Goupil?"[45]

Durand-Ruel became increasingly irritated with Theo's progress, and with all the artists who were now working with him. In a letter to his son, Pissarro tells how the dealer reacted when he learned that Pissarro was in negotiations with Theo: "Durand [sic] took me aside and asked me if I had taken any paintings to Theo van Gogh. 'Yes,' I replied. 'You shouldn't,' he said to me, 'take paintings to that devil of a man! . . . Bring them to me, and especially don't do business with Theo van Gogh, because as long as he has paintings of yours, that'll hurt my business and make it impossible for me to sell any.' . . . So I told him very frankly that since Theo van Gogh had sold some of my new canvases, and thought they were very good, and represented them intelligently, I couldn't take back what I had left with him."[46]

Theo, who was becoming serious competition for Durand-Ruel, persevered doggedly. As agreed, he bought ten paintings from Monet and immediately organized an exhibition that included landscapes of the Breton and Mediterranean coasts and Dutch tulip fields. All of Monet's paintings shown by Theo between 1888 and 1889 sold, a financial coup made all the more significant because Monet's works were fetching larger sums. A German painter, Hermann Schlittgen, who went to the gallery to see the exhibition, writes of meeting Theo: "A likable young gallery assistant with red hair, who didn't look French, soon began greeting us as if we were longtime acquaintances. . . . We had formed the habit of looking at the canvases and admiring them, while the young man said nothing, smiling, with a satisfied air. After a few days, he addressed us, saying that he saw we were interested in modern art and that he had a brother who was a painter who lived in the country, and asking our permission to show us some of his paintings. The young man stayed modestly to one side, watching what effect was produced. . . . We were still under Monet's charm and a little perplexed. This was something entirely different: nature seen through a forceful, decorative will; sometimes the contours were outlined in blue, as in Japanese prints. The young man asked my opinion. I praised the fine, pure color, even though overall the painting was too stylized for my taste. He thanked us in a friendly way and took back his canvases. After that, whenever we passed by the gallery, he would often watch us through the glass door and smile to us when he saw us. Much later we learned that his name was Theo van Gogh."[47]

Although Theo actively promoted the paintings of the Impressionists and Post-Impressionists, he was always more reticent when it came to Vincent's work. This may have been because Vincent was his brother, or because Vincent, unlike the others, enjoyed a certain financial security. Certainly,

FIG. 2: Vincent van Gogh, *Gardens on Montmartre*, 1887.
Stedelijk, Amsterdam

Theo wished to avoid angering his employers. He did eventually sell one of Vincent's paintings to the Sully & Lory gallery in 1888.[48] Then he suggested to his brother that he show his canvases at the annual Impressionist exhibition.

Vincent was very busy with his work in Arles, so Theo showed three paintings from Vincent's Paris period: *Romans parisiens*, *Gardens on Montmartre* (fig. 2), and *Behind the Moulin de la Galette*.

In the spring of 1888, the young art dealer sent Impressionist paintings to Holland—a first—and slipped a few of Vincent's recent canvases in with them. Tersteeg's reaction was implacable: he wanted nothing to do with the paintings, considering them the work of painters suffering from advanced delirium. Confronted with such intolerance and lack of understanding, Theo was again terribly discouraged. He did not comprehend the art world's hostility toward many examples of the new painting, and blamed himself for not being able to do more for these misunderstood artists. Vincent reassures him: "I wish I could manage to make you really understand that when you give money to artists, you are yourself doing an artist's work, and that I only want my pictures to be of such a quality that you will not be too dissatisfied with your work."[49] Vincent always returned to this idea of a common endeavor, in which both brothers shared equally: in his letters, he often used the phrases "our paintings," and "our work."

Vincent had been making progress in his work ever since arriving in Arles. He had made many paintings of flowers, of trees, and of the Langlois bridge, which reminded him of home, and had painted portraits of friends, such as Paul-Eugène Milliet, a second lieutenant in the Zouaves, and the mail carrier Joseph Roulin. He executed series—orchards in white and pink, wheat fields, and sowers. He adorned his studio with paintings of sunflowers. Hearing of the death of the painter Anton Mauve, after finishing a painting of a flowering peach tree, he wrote on the picture, "In memory of Mauve, Theo and Vincent." He also undertook various versions of *The Starry Night*. His style was evolving. Away from Paris, he moved away from Impressionism. His brushstrokes became more sure and aggressive; he sought to heighten colors and simplify forms. He painted frenziedly for hours, sometimes into the night, when he would wear lit candles on his straw hat. In early June, he moved into a small yellow house. But he was lonely. Seeing his brother successfully introducing the new generation of painters in Paris, he wished that he, too, could assemble a small community of artists in Arles.

Missing the endless conversations about art he had enjoyed in Paris, Vincent asked Gauguin to join him in the Midi. Vincent so admired the man, his spirit, and his creativity, that he nagged Theo to press their friend to come live with him, but Gauguin was in no hurry to leave Pont-Aven.

The death of their uncle Cent, however, proved to be fortuitous. Theo inherited a large sum of money on his uncle's death. To make his lonely brother happy, he proposed to Gauguin to send him 150 francs a month, in exchange for one painting a month on the condition that he move to Arles. In addition, Theo would pay his travel expenses to Arles. Gauguin, who had money problems, accepted the offer, but dawdled, giving various excuses. He finally arrived on October 23, to Vincent's great joy.

It was not long before conflicts between the two emerged, in particular around their artistic points of view. Their relationship and friendship gradually deteriorated: daily quarrels and suspicions spoiled what Vincent had hoped would be a congenial atmosphere. The incompatibility of their temperaments was glaring.

Theo thus found himself with two painters under contract—something he had not really intended—and playing the role both of patron and dealer. But he was treated poorly in spite of his generosity: Gauguin had agreed to the arrangement out of self-interest, and the tone of his letters remained haughty and distant. Theo was hurt by his attitude; he was, after all, very sensitive to Gauguin's work and talked about it very well: "You will remember Gauguin's paintings," he writes Wil, "which express a strange poetry. He has made some new pictures down south. Winter landscapes, with delicate green hills against a rust-colored sky. And spring-time landscapes with trees with very fine branches, on which the leaves look like little bells delighting in nature's renewed youth. . . . In a way, Gauguin murmurs words of consolation to those who are unhappy or in poor health."[50]

In his letters to Wil, Theo also spoke of himself, suggesting, however indirectly, that he was not at all well. He suffered from anxiety, and had always had serious health problems. Overall fatigue was giving him a wan look. When Vincent learned of this, he was concerned; he warned Theo to follow his doctor's advice to the letter.

Besides his health problems, Theo was experiencing stress at work, subjected as he was to Boussod and Valadon's criticism and mockery, arising from their disapproval of Theo's promotion of artists with little commercial prospects. Beyond their differences from a purely aesthetic standpoint, the principal issues were money and the works' profit-making potential. The numbers did not lie: where a painting by Renoir might sell—with difficulty—for 150 francs, one of Gérôme's canvases, *A Street in Cairo*, purchased for 50,000 francs in 1887, sold for 70,000 francs to a rich American two years later.[51] A portrait of Madame Van Loon by Cabanel, bought for 27,000 francs, sold for 30,000 francs. The profit margin was the same for Jules Dupré's works. In 1887, Chauchard, the director of the department store La Samaritaine, acquired two canvases by Dupré for 24,500 francs and 20,000 francs, respectively. In 1889, at a sale in the United States, a painting by Jean-Louis-Ernest Meissonier reached a price of $71,000. That same year, Durand-Ruel was forced to liquidate his stock in New York. He received $675 for a painting by Renoir, and $400 for a Degas pastel. Pissarro's and Sisley's works went for $200 apiece. Only Monet's canvases found buyers at "proper" prices—around 1,000 francs. Given this reality, Boussod and Valadon considered it madness to fight so hard for paintings that sold for ridiculous prices. Theo's position was tenuous, because he was not free to extend his sphere of action or to make the decisions he wished. His employers kept an eye on him; for example, one or the other often accompanied him when he went to Giverny to discuss business with Monet.

During this period in late 1888, Theo was depressed. Besides the work problems that gnawed at him, he had quarreled with his closest friend, Andries. A chill had come between them after Andries had offered to lend Theo money to open a gallery, but then reneged. Matters were only made worse by the presence of Annie van der Linden, Dries's wife, whom Theo did not like.

Feeling distressed and alone, Theo succumbed to despair. All he wanted was the quiet happiness of a simple, serene life, and he felt his only hope was to make a home and find stability with a wife. He had chosen the woman some time ago; now he waited for her to return his feelings, sadly in vain.

5 LIFE WITH JOHANNA

1888-1890

"**G**UESS WHO I BUMPED INTO here a couple of days ago, Jo Bonger, whatever was I to do? . . . First she wanted to know whether it was her fault that I no longer socialized with André [Andries]. One subject led to another and we were on such informal terms I thought I could treat her amicably, and I became good friends with her & her brother once again. But mother, that was impossible, I loved her too much, & now that we have seen one another a great deal these last few days, she has told me she loves me too & that she will take me the way I am. I am actually very worried that she is making a mistake & that she will be disappointed in me, but I am so very happy, & I shall try my best to make her happy, if I can. If I am perhaps giving you the idea that ours was a chance meeting, then that is

Johanna Bonger, 1862–1925

wrong of me, for it was she who arranged the meeting with a great deal of tact, & noble feeling, otherwise it would never have happened. I do believe that she knew that I still loved her beforehand. And now dear Mother I ask you to take her into your loving mother's heart. . . . O Mother I am so inexpressibly happy. Can it really be true?"[1]

Theo was rarely so euphoric in his letters. He had loved Jo Bonger secretly since meeting her in Holland in 1885. But his love had come to naught—she was involved with another man. He had given up any hope of a relationship with her when, by complete surprise, he ran into her on the street in Paris. Jo was spending several days in the city visiting her brother. And after a few hours of catching up, Jo felt confident enough to tell Theo that she shared his feelings.

Although his rapture filled his letters, his lack of self-confidence is also very evident. He feared he would be unable to make her truly happy. Theo suffered from self-doubt his entire life, and this turn of events only exacerbated these feelings.

He turned to his mother for encouragement, as he had when he was younger. Her reply was joyful and revealed her understanding of his longing for a wife: "You know that I have always believed that you have a good destiny for your own household. I have known since your childhood that you were sensitive to the idea of the simple happiness of your own home."[2] (This conception of love as a simple happiness, somewhere between romantic passion and bourgeois simplicity, was very popular in France in the latter half of the nineteenth century.[3] Theo believed in it completely.)

Anna was careful not to encourage Theo too much, as she knew little about the intentions of the young woman's family. And though she was not overly enthusiastic, she was very positive about Jo: "Say to her [Jo] that I hope everything works out for your happiness. Assure her that I will welcome her and I want to make her acquaintance. I will love her as much as I love you. . . . I also hope that her parents will accept you as you have accepted their child."[4]

Theo was happy: for him, Jo embodied eternally feminine traits, and he saw in her rare and precious qualities. And they shared a common background, which only enhanced the ease with which they dealt with each other. It was unlikely that Theo, a nineteenth-century Dutchman, could have had the kind of marriage he dreamed of with a Frenchwoman. He laments this as early as 1887, in a letter to his sister Lies: "I don't remember when I wrote you last and if I have already told you my secret. To get straight to the point, if you don't know yet; I am planning at one time or another to ask for Jo Bonger's hand. I surely don't know her enough to be able to tell you much about her. As you know, I have only seen her a few times, but the things I know about her appeal to me. She gives me the impression that I could trust her in a completely undefinable way, more than anyone else. I think I could talk with her about anything."[5]

Johanna Gesina Bonger was a gentle, intelligent, and cultured woman. Born on October 4, 1862, in Amsterdam, she was the fifth of seven children. Her father, Hendrik Christiaan Bonger, worked for an insurance company, while her mother, Hermine Louise Weissman, raised the children.[6] Jo was a happy child, and, by all accounts, easy to get along with. Andries, a year older, was clearly her favorite sibling. Raised in an educated, music-loving family, Jo shared the family's affection for music and cherished the "quartet" evenings that her father organized.[7]

With a gift for the English language, she enrolled in the

university in Amsterdam and earned her A and B diplomas, which allowed her to teach English. She was sent to London for a few months to perfect her English, and there she worked at the British Museum Library. She was to prepare a monograph for her examination, and elected to write on Percy Shelley, the English poet and playwright whose turbulent life and scandalous affairs eclipsed for a time the quality of his uniquely lyrical and musical verses. She would long remain enthralled by the magic of his poetry. Another author she was equally drawn to was the contemporary Dutch writer Multatuli (Eduard Douwes Dekker), with his heroic conduct and eventful life. Jo was attracted to adventurers and rebels; her special sensitivity toward creative and original personalities naturally inclined her to be sympathetic to Vincent. Since Vincent was such an important part of Theo's life, it was essential his partner understand his difficult older brother.

Her brief teaching career began in 1886 at a girls' boarding school in Tilburg; she was then hired by a Utrecht high school. She devoted herself to her work. Toward the end of her engagement to Theo, in March 1889, she described her intellectual evolution: "There was a time when my only ambition was to study, to be clever, to know everything (at the very least). That was my ideal . . . I lived in my books up to a point where I felt it wasn't right—that that wasn't really *life*. . . . My period in Elburg [Jo Bonger taught at a girls' school in Elburg for a year] was what I would call a time of 'pleasant reality.' I was doing something, not within what I had learnt, I was somebody in that small circle, but in the long run it was too confined and parochial. Then there was a time in A[msterdam], when I felt I ought to go out 'into the world'—see lots of people, get about, be up-to-date on everything, in a word, an ordinary person, but that too proved unsatisfying in the long run. And finally, having gone through one stage and another, I learnt that happiness, the aim of life, is not something distant but actually very close. . . ."[8]

Jo's youthful features were typically Dutch—very simple, almost plain. She wore her brown hair pulled back, except for wispy bangs that framed her broad face. Johanna's uniqueness was a result of her subtle mix of masculinity—her rather coarse features—and femininity—the soft curves of her body and milky cheeks. She dressed quietly, adding a brooch or other accessory to her bodice to set off the simplicity of her clothes.

Jo made a good impression on Anna, who praised her diplomatic abilities in the reconciliation between Theo and Andries: "I saw your Jo once, and found her very sweet and very good-hearted. She had a very good manner about her. What you told me about her before made her not seem like a stranger."[9]

THEO HAD GREAT HOPES FOR THE UNION: "I think that if she wished it so she could be so much to me. . . . You girls usually think that the world is full of all kinds of heroes and that the man who asks you to marry him belongs to that category of beings. I find that very fine, and would not wish to disillusion you, but I think more than one of you is mistaken if she counts on it. . . . I would not like to be taken for someone I am not," he complains in a letter to Lies. He adds that he would like Jo to know him well, so that she might not have too many illusions, then ends with: "And indeed, there is still some question about whether she will accept me. Yet I cannot keep my thoughts away from her, she is always with me."[10]

At thirty-one years old, Theo spoke of the future with the anxiety and uncertainty of an adolescent. He felt the need to confide in women close to him, chiefly his mother and his sister Lies. In December 1888, when his plans took an unexpected turn, he writes to Lies, not Vincent: "You are one of the first to whom I am going to tell this great news that means a great turning point that is making me inexpressibly happy. . . . I've gotten engaged to Jo Bonger. I write it, but I can't manage to realize that it's the truth, after believing so little time ago that it would never happen. It's difficult to tell you precisely how everything happened, because I don't exactly know myself anymore. She has been living with her brother for four weeks. She was just about to leave when I ran into her. We saw each other again, and I very quickly noticed that I loved her as much as I did before. Now we understand each other better. . . . She is a noble and sweet girl, in whom I have the greatest trust. If only I could make her happy—as she expects me to—I'll do my best. It would be a gift to all of us. For if my disorderly life ceases, I hope that we will all be a little closer. Next Wednesday, she goes to Amsterdam, and I think that I'll finally be able to go on January 1 and announce our engagement. If it were possible, I'd think it fantastic if you could come, too, so that we could see each other. I only hope that you will love her. It is my desire and hers, too. I hope that Jo will write you soon. Today, I hope to receive a letter from Papa and Mama Bonger, and from our mother as well, and I already know that there will be no great obstacle, because I've received a telegram from her brother Henry."[11]

Theo was happy—and relieved—that one of his future brothers-in-law approved, because for some days the hostility of Dries's wife, Annie, was threatening the promise of their happiness. He shares this with his mother: "It is possible that Jo will leave on Monday, because Andrie's wife resents us for some unknown reason. And if that doesn't work out, it would be better for her to go home, even though I would have liked to have kept her here."[12] He would have preferred to leave for Amsterdam with Jo, as planned, asked for her hand right away, then introduced his future bride to his mother. Unfortunately, work prevented him from leaving Paris, so he made his request by letter and announced his arrival for the first days of January 1889. His high spirits were short-lived. Just as his happiness with Jo was within reach, he received a devastating telegram regarding his brother.

Problems in Arles

"CHRISTMAS EVENING—Theo and I had just become engaged and meant to go to Holland together—a telegram arrived calling Theo to Arles. The evening of December 23, in an attack of violent overexcitement, an access of high fever with delirium, Vincent had cut off a part of his ear and had taken it to a woman in a brothel; there was a great ruckus, Roulin the post-office employee had taken Vincent home, the police had gotten involved; they had found Vincent bleeding and fainted in bed and had taken him to the hospital."[13] Several years after the catastrophe, this was how Jo described the events of those tragically famous days. Vincent's self-portrait painted after the incident is one of his most well-known paintings (fig. 1).

At the yellow house, Vincent and Gauguin were finding it difficult to live together. The latter complains to Theo in a letter: "Everything considered, I am obliged to return to Paris. Vincent and I simply cannot live together without trouble, due to the incompatibility of our characters, and we both need tranquility for our work. He is a man of remarkable intelligence whom I esteem very highly and whom I

Fig. 1: Vincent van Gogh, *Self-portrait with Bandaged Ear*, 1889. Courtauld Institute, London

leave with regret, but I must repeat, it is necessary that I leave."[14] Vincent had already realized that his grand plan for a "studio of the South" was shattering. Once again an unbearable loneliness was swallowing him up. Unable to resign himself to this, he tried to keep Gauguin from going, but to no avail. Bernard reported what Gauguin had told him in a letter to Albert Aurier, a young critic and journalist: "Ever since the question arose of my leaving Arles he had been so queer that I hardly breathed anymore. He even said to me: 'You are going to leave,' and when I said, 'Yes,' he tore a sentence from a newspaper and put it in my hand: '*The murderer has fled.*'"[15]

On December 23, Gauguin went to take the air after dinner. He heard irregular steps behind him: "The day before I left [Arles] Vincent ran after me—it was at night—and I turned around, for Vincent had been behaving strangely for some time and I was on my guard. He then said to me: 'You are taciturn, but I shall be likewise.' I went to sleep in a hotel and when I returned the entire population of Arles was in front of our house."[16] A few years later, Gauguin explained that Vincent had threatened him with a razor, though the exact events of that night are not known. Historians believe that Vincent went home and, tormented by auditory hallucinations, cut off part of his left ear. He then wrapped his head in a towel to stop the bleeding, donned a cap, cleaned off the piece of cut flesh, wrapped it up, went to the brothel he and Gauguin frequented, and offered it to Rachel, a young prostitute. After giving her the packet and telling her, "Treasure this," Vincent went home to bed. The next morning, Gauguin learned what had happened— from the policeman who had been in the wounded man's bed-room—and he immediately fled to Paris, after informing Theo by telegram. Theo was needed in Arles immediately.

Theo left Jo, who was still living at her brother's, a brief message: "Vincent is gravely ill. I don't know what's wrong, but I shall have to go there as my presence is required. I'm so sorry that you will be upset because of me, when instead I would like to make you happy. . . . I shall keep up my spirits by thinking of you."[17] He knew neither the gravity of the situation nor the details. On Christmas Eve, Jo accompanied her fiancé to the train station, where, on the freezing platform, he boarded the train to Arles, and on the morning of December 25, found himself at his unconscious brother's bedside. Theo, devastated, thought Vincent was dying.

"The prospect of losing my brother, who has meant so much to me & has become so much a part of me, made me realize what a terrible emptiness I would feel if he were no longer there. . . . Will he remain insane? The doctors think it possible, but daren't yet say for certain. . . . He seemed to be all right for a few minutes when I was with him, but lapsed shortly afterwards into his brooding about philosophy & theology. It was terribly sad being there, because from time to time all his grief would well up inside & he would try to weep, but couldn't. Poor fighter & poor, poor sufferer. Nothing can be done to relieve his anguish now, but it is deep & hard for him to bear. Had he just once found someone to whom he could pour his heart out, it might never have come to this."[18]

A shattered Theo took the train back to Paris. His presence did nothing for Vincent, who was too addled. Roulin, the postal employee and faithful friend of the painter, and Félix Rey, a physician at the hospital in Arles, would keep him informed about his brother's health.

"Since I last wrote I've been wavering between hope & fear. The news is still bad. . . . There is little hope, but he has done more than so many in his life & suffered & fought more than most people are capable of doing. If he must pass away, so be it, but the thought of it breaks my heart. Dearest Jo, I cannot speak my mind like this to anyone else & I thank you for it. . . . Though the life I am offering you may not be carefree, together we shall try to see the sunlight as well as the storms."[19] Jo read his letter with great attention and supported Theo as best she could. She was essential to him during this difficult time.

Theo was wracked by these latest events: just when he should have been concentrating on building his future home—Hendrik Christiaan Bonger granted him his daughter's hand in a letter Theo received on December 30—he was overwhelmed by the situation in Arles. His happiness with Jo was marred by Vincent's condition: "I so long to be with you that I shall not postpone it for a single day unless I absolutely must: there's still a risk. . . . I almost dare not hope for his complete recovery, because the attack was the culmination of a variety of things that have been pushing him in that direction over a long period of time. All one can hope for is that his suffering is brief. When I mentioned you to him he evidently knew who & what I meant & when I asked whether he approved of our plans, he said yes, but that marriage ought not to be regarded as the main object in life."[20] For Vincent, the only matter of major importance was, obviously, his art. His only reason for living, and his chief defense against a fatal drifting, was the project the two of them were creating, "that one gives so that the other may receive, while one provides what it takes to pursue it, and that, in these exchanges, it will never be clear who is taking, who is giving, or even, really, who is painting."[21]

Despite his condition, Vincent understood that, in choosing a "real life"—the domestic life that Vincent was not made for, and that Theo had secretly dreamed of for years—

his brother was leaving him behind. He was terrified by the introduction of a third person in their lives. He feared nothing would ever be the same again, and that his brother would unintentionally withdraw from his social and material role, which was necessary to Vincent's survival. The two brothers lived in genuine symbiosis; the word, used by the Dutch professor G. Kraus and the French psychoanalyst Charles Mauron, described, in Mauron's words, "that the bond joining the two brothers was something more vital and more functional than mere mutual affection, no matter how heartfelt."[22] Separated from his brother because of the love that Theo felt for Jo, Vincent would be unable to survive. The inexorable process of destruction was set in motion.

As for Theo, he thought Vincent was dying. He accepted the situation with sorrow and resignation. Jo was there to assuage his grief. Besides his fiancée's love, another consolation would be achieving a post-mortem acknowledgment of his brother's work. Theo writes to Jo, in 1889, as though Vincent had already died: "You know how much he has meant to me & that it was he who fostered and nurtured whatever good there might be in me. . . . I would have wanted him, whether near or far, to remain that same advisor & brother. . . . [B]ut it goes to show yet again that one must rely on oneself. We shall honor his memory, shan't we, dearest?"[23]

He continues to confide in Jo: "For even now, I sense from the letters from home that their words of sympathy, all except Wil's, barely disguise their conviction that he was actually insane all along. Here, Degas, Gauguin & Andries are the only people in my circle who do not share this view & who have supported me through this period. But no one has done as much for me as you my dearest."[24]

As for Vincent's supposed madness, Wil's and Emile

Bernard's letters confirm Theo's feelings. Wil, sorrowfully compassionate, asked her brother to conceal nothing about the medical diagnosis, and offered to send him the money—which she held—representing Vincent's share of their inheritance, to cover the medical costs. She also promised to travel to see him if he were dying. Bernard appeared sincerely shocked to hear of Vincent's hospitalization: "My best friend, my dear friend Vincent is mad. Since I have found out, I am almost mad myself. . . . My dear friend is lost and it will probably be only a question of time until his approaching death!."[25] Bernard had been informed by Gauguin of Vincent's situation.

Against all expectation, Vincent recovered. His condition no longer required him to be in isolation. Beginning December 29, he was under treatment in the hospital's common ward. At Theo's request, Pastor Salles was now attending him. Theo expresses his relief in a letter to his fiancée: "He [Vincent] has calmed down and there is a chance that everything will come right again. If the outbursts have been beneficial & he stops making such extraordinary demands of himself, who knows, it may have done him good to let off steam."[26] The rest of his missive concerns only Jo, their future life, their plans, and their feelings: "There's no reason now to postpone my arrival any longer & I shall be overjoyed to be with you again. . . . [N]ow, after the haze of the past few days, in which I was so preoccupied with Vincent & busy at work, I feel a great emptiness when you're not there."[27]

He left immediately, getting on the first train for Holland, to be with his beloved. Their marriage was officially announced, and they exchanged wedding rings even before the ceremony. Theo, who was warmly received by his future in-laws, was blissful. Vincent learned of the good news from a wedding card that Jo made sure he received. His congratulations, in turn, were laconic.

THE WEDDING WAS PLANNED FOR MARCH OR APRIL, in Amsterdam. As Theo and Jo impatiently awaited the happy day, they began to know each other, and their passions, better through letters.

Art, of course, was one of the most important things in Theo's life. At the same time, his position as an art dealer gave him an ambiguous status. On the one hand, he was not a businessman, possessed by the desire for money and profit— as his employers quite frequently pointed out. On the other hand, he was not an artist: he did not create art himself, but merely supported those who did create it. There was a certain distance between painting and himself. "I would be so glad if you were also to love artists & their work," he writes his fiancée. "It's marvelous to see how the finest products of the human heart are born & how they affect the lives of so many people."[28] In his every letter to her, he writes succinctly about painting and the effects of art on humanity. Gauguin, Pissarro, Monet, and all the artists he believed in are often mentioned in his correspondence and the correspondence reveals his admiration of them and their work. He tells Jo he would like to talk about art frequently with her, "because it touches my life more than anything else. Dries and I never see eye to eye on it. He regarded art as something marvelous, but not as anything to do with life itself. He feels the greatest work of art is one where the most difficulties have been overcome, whereas I don't believe the execution is so important, as long as it comes straight from the heart. The form of art is not art itself. Nor did it use to be regarded as such, but then painting didn't use to have such an impact on our lives."[29]

However, his main concern was always Vincent, a pre-occupation chronicled in his many letters to Jo. When she asks about Vincent's health, Theo replies that he fears that "Vincent is not completely normal yet,"[30] and that he encounters more difficulties than he should. Theo had no intention of abandoning his brother, but the path he suggested to Vincent was one he was incapable of following.

Vincent had already written him early that month: "I have read and re-read your letter about your meeting with the Bongers. It is perfect. As for me, I am content to stay just as I am."[31] How bitterly he must have received Theo's advice to follow his brother's example of finding a wife and settling down. Theo, somewhat thoughtlessly, hoped to share his joy with his brother by telling him in great detail of his happy domestic situation: Anna and their sisters were getting along marvelously with his fiancée; Wil and Jo wrote each other and sent each other little presents. In a letter dated March 8, Wil confided in her future sister-in-law how much she loved her.[32] The van Goghs were deeply touched by Jo's compassion toward Vincent, and Anna immediately wrote Theo that Jo was a great comfort in their grief.[33] Anna acted as mediator between the two regarding questions of their future household, or Jo's marital anxieties.

Theo was profoundly saddened by the impossibility of sharing his joy with his brother: "You have done so much for me that it is a great sorrow for me to know that, precisely at this time when in all probability I am going to have days of happiness with my dear Jo, you are passing through days of misery."[34]

After he came out of the hospital, Vincent had trouble living both with himself and with those around him. Back in the yellow house, the auditory hallucinations resumed, combined with the paranoia that someone was trying to poison him. People from his neighborhood, convinced that as long as he was free he posed a threat, organized a petition, a result of which caused Vincent to be arrested and again committed in Arles. Roulin, Rey, and Salles stayed close to him; Theo continued to send him money, but made no travel plans. The ticket was expensive, but he was also loathe to see his brother so sick. "I'm almost inclined to go back there myself, but it would serve no purpose & be no less distressing than the first time I went," he writes Jo. [35]

Seeking reassurance of his brother's well-being, Theo persuaded Paul Signac to stop in Arles on March 23 on his way to Cassis. The visit went well—until Vincent tried to swallow a bottle of turpentine immediately after showing his friend his most recent canvases. Signac left him in the care of his doctors and sent Theo a report of what had happened.

A week later, on Saturday, March 30 (Vincent's birthday), Theo boarded a train for Holland to see his fiancée and organize their wedding, which was set for April 18 at the Amsterdam town hall (fig. 2).

Neither Theo nor his fiancée saw any reason for a religious ceremony. Wil begs him to reconsider, to make the family happy: "Moe worries day and night about your not being married in church. For home, for the Bonger family, it's just out of the question. Come on, do it, otherwise it will make everyone miserable. You can arrange the reception and all of that, otherwise it will be impossible. You can do it without genuflecting. You know that can be done, you just have to ask the pastor. And that would make it just a wish for happiness, because in any case you're not in the world for your own pleasure. So, do it." [36]

Faced with both families' insistence, Theo succumbed

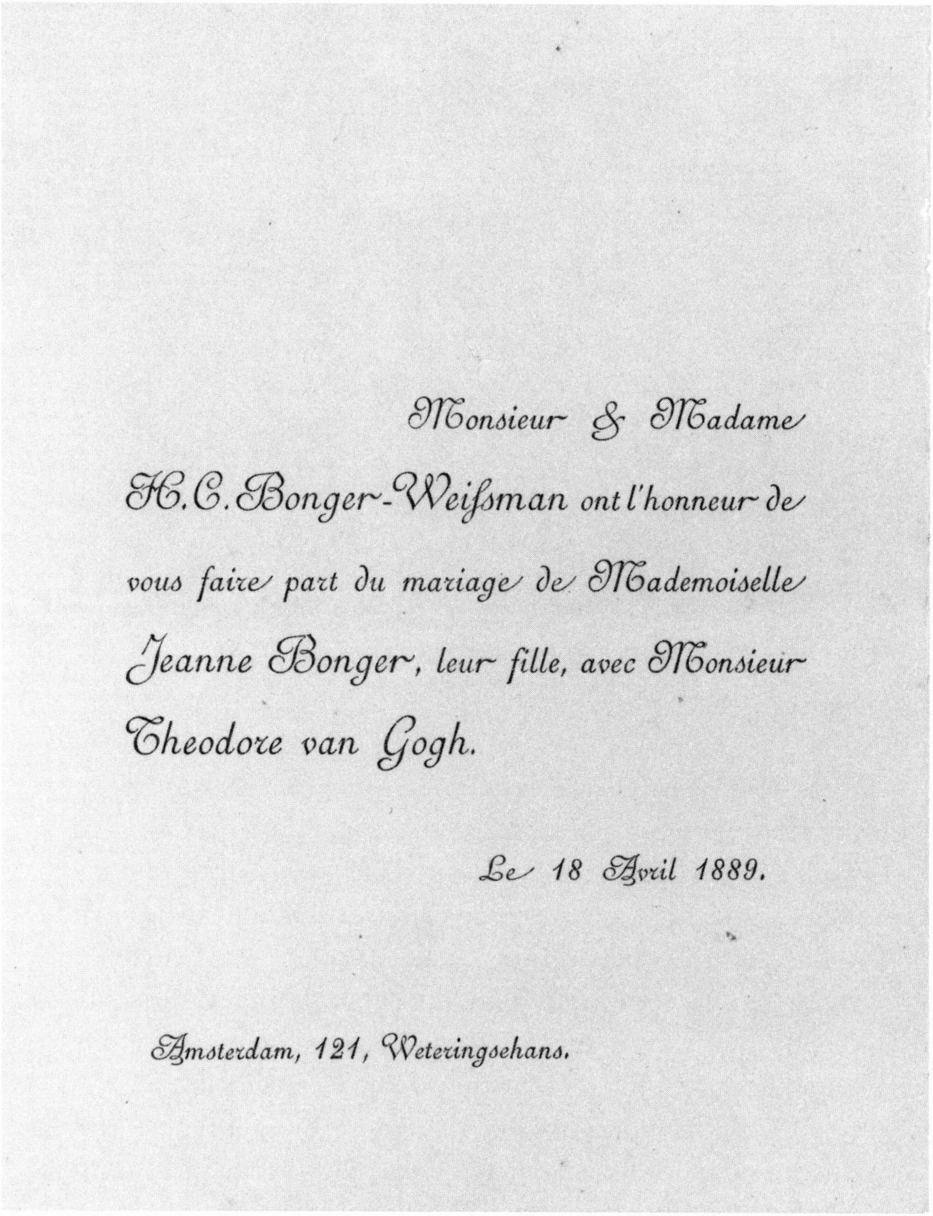

Monsieur & Madame
H.C. Bonger-Weißman ont l'honneur de
vous faire part du mariage de Mademoiselle
Jeanne Bonger, leur fille, avec Monsieur
Theodore van Gogh.

Le 18 Avril 1889.

Amsterdam, 121, Weteringschans.

FIG. 2: *Announcement of the wedding of Theo van Gogh
and Johanna Bonger, April 18, 1889*

FIG. 3: *The entry of Theo and Jo's apartment building on Cité Pigalle as it looks today.*

to the pressure, at least initially. "It does look as if we shall be married in church after all, as the argument I put forward wasn't taken into consideration. Don't you agree that we should do so to please everyone? But I shan't hide the fact that I consider it a farce. It is not a shame that however firm one's views may be, one cannot always persuade others to share them. . . . It's most unfortunate."[37] Though he did speak his mind, he lacked the wherewithal to impose his ideas.

At this point in his relatively young life, he was exhausted in every way: psychologically, by the incessant professional struggles and conflicted relations with his brother and physically, because he had been consumed by illness for years. Though he was happy about his impending marriage, life itself had become a constant source of anxiety for him. Johanna was trying to restore his faith in life and attempting to teach him how to experience some sense of peace in the midst of his troubles, and he was grateful for her help: "There will be difficulties, my dear child, but with you I feel the strength to overcome them," he writes her. "I live in a fog. I have not been able to be myself lately. [But] . . . the most important thing is love, and I love you madly."[38]

As for the wedding, their original plan to be wed in a civil ceremony was back on. Anna and the Bongers respected their children's wishes: it would take place only at the Amsterdam town hall, on the date planned, in a very intimate gathering. Only friends and family were invited, except for Vincent, whose health did not allow him to travel.

Immediately after the ceremony, the newlyweds left Holland for their new apartment on Cité Pigalle (fig. 3). Upon his arrival in Paris, on April 19, Theo found a letter from Pastor Salles with news of recent developments: Vincent still refused to live in Rey's small apartment, preferring to remain in a situation where he was entirely taken care of. He felt he had neither the heart nor the strength to live alone. Frequent fainting spells made him tired and rendered him temporarily amnesiac: "He is entirely conscious of his condition and talks to me of what he has been through and which he fears may return, with a candor and simplicity which [are] touching. 'I am not able,' he told me the day before yesterday, 'to look after myself and control myself; I feel quite different from what I used to be.' . . . He has, therefore, requested that I obtain the necessary particulars, in order that he may be admitted somewhere and also to write to you in this sense. Considering this decision, taken after mature deliberation, I thought that, before turning to you, I would obtain some information regarding a private institution near Arles, at Saint-Remy, where it appears that the inmates are very well treated. I send you the reply which I have received and the prospectus that came with it."[39] Theo, terribly upset by his brother's decision, which he interpreted as a sign that Vincent was giving up, writes him in an attempt to reassure him: "Let's hope that this is meant only as a preventative measure. Seeing that I know you well enough to consider you capable of all imaginable sacrifices, I have been contemplating the possibility that you have thought of this solution in order to inconvenience less those who know you. If this should be the case, I implore you not to do it, for life in such an establishment can hardly be pleasant."[40] Theo also suggests that Vincent go to Pont-Aven, or come to Paris for a while.

THEO HAD LONG BEEN AWARE that Vincent's personality was very complex. Shortly before his wedding, when Jo had proposed that they take in her future brother-in-law in Paris, Theo explained: "Indeed, one of the main problems is that, whether sick or well, his life is so barren in terms of what he gets from outside. But if you knew him, you would appreciate twice as much how hard it is to solve the problem of what must & what can be done. As you know, he abandoned what they call *convenances* [conventions] a long time ago. From his style of dress & his demeanor you can see at once that he is different & for years everyone who sees him has said *C'est un fou* [He's a madman]. I don't mind that at all, but at home it is not acceptable. Then there's something in the way he talks that makes people either love him very dearly or unable to tolerate him. He is always surrounded by people who are attracted to him, but also by lots of enemies. He cannot be detached in his dealings with people, It is either one thing or the other. Even those with whom he is the best of friends find him difficult to get along with, as he spares nothing and no one. . . . If I had time, I should go and see him & go hiking with him, for instance. That is the only thing I can think of that would really give him peace of mind. If one of those painters might like to do that, I shall send him there. But those he gets on with are slightly afraid of him, which Gauguin's visit to him did nothing to change, on the contrary."[41]

Theo was tired of sacrificing himself for his brother, and he longed to go on with his life with Jo. He had already told Jo that the frenetic energy of Paris did not suit Vincent, and there were obstacles to working—the police would not let him stop where he wished to paint, and models refused to pose for him. Now, he had neither the strength nor the desire to repeat the experience. Nonetheless, he continued to feel bad for Vincent's suffering: "It's distressing to be so powerless to do anything for him, but exceptional people need exceptional remedies & I only hope they will yet be found where ordinary people would not look."[42]

Vincent, meanwhile, was worried and agitated. Theo reassured him, telling him his monthly stipend was well deserved: ". . . really, you are making far too much of something which is entirely natural, without taking into account that you have repaid me many times over, by your work as well as by your friendship, which is of greater value than all the money I shall ever possess."[43] Generously, Theo refers not to the money he was giving Vincent, but to what he could earn from the selling of his work. To cheer him up, Theo shared with him the charms of married life: ". . . the apartment looks more lived in every day, thanks to all sorts of inventions of Jo's. We thoroughly understand each other, so we feel such a complete mutual satisfaction that we feel happier than I should say. . . . I never dared hope for so much happiness."[44]

The Young Couple's Life in Paris

While Theo was busy at the gallery, Jo devoted herself to organizing their lives, and getting their apartment in order. It was on the fourth floor, and Theo did not entirely like it, finding "the foyer in poor condition, the kitchen dark . . . [and] the neighborhood not very chic," whereas Jo was content. The dining room became the living room while the living room was being worked on. Theo, with his fine aesthetic sense, wished to dress the windows with rare Indonesian weavings of yellow-blue silk. Their home also had three rooms that were sunny "from nine in the morning until six in the evening," as Jo describes in a letter to her family. She meticulously described each room, including the cellar where Theo stored their cask of wine and their coal. She described her relationship with the maid—who was not very tidy—and lamented that she played the piano less assiduously than before. Her letters reveal a comfortable, bourgeois life. Jo dutifully fulfilled her role as a wife, taking on certain household chores, such as washing the silver they used at every meal, and having the servant "prepare potatoes in the Dutch way."

Theo settled into domestic life, and left behind his Bohemian existence—there were no more nights out in Montmartre. The van Goghs preferred entertaining and socializing at home: the painters Isaäcson and Hart Nibbrig dined there from time to time, and often stopped by, and they often spent evenings with Andries and the Pissarros.

The painter and his son, Lucien, were already regular visitors at Jo and Theo's apartment; the neighbors recognized this large man, with his thick white beard, soft felt hat, and black raincoat, and he was always accompanied by a young man who strongly resembled him. Nicknamed by his friends alternately as "Moses," "Abraham," and "God," Pissarro displayed a goodness as impressive as his physical strength. At fifty-nine years old, he had lost none of his revolutionary ardor. A dedicated anarchist in the Pierre Joseph Proudhon mold, he militated for class struggle: "When will there be a proper revolution, when every bourgeois will be forced to buy at least two pictures from artists every year in perpetuity?"[45] Frightened by his subversive ideas, Monet, Sisley, Gauguin, and Renoir preferred to keep their distance, but Theo continued to see him, attracted as he was by the painter's generous spirit. Jo, equally charmed, listened to him in silence when he came to visit. She had long held the same opinions, but, too shy to express herself in French, she was content to nod as he spoke.

After the parties, Jo and Theo were alone again at last, tired but happy in their married solitude: "You know, during the day we haven't time to do our errands together, and at night, when Theo finally gets home, we'd rather stay in."[46] They did experience Paris at night, however, and Jo was discovering the city with pleasure: "Every now and then, we go out on the town most astonishingly. On Tuesday, M. Tersteeg came to eat here, and reciprocated by asking us to dine with him at the Doyen, a restaurant on the Champs-Elysées, outdoors . . . it's really very enjoyable. It was a truly pleasant evening. . . ."[47] Other times they would go to the restaurant at the Tour Eiffel, as the guests of Vittorio-Matteo Corcos, an Italian painter who was a friend of Theo.

Before long, Jo made up her mind to write Vincent: "When we were not yet married I was always thinking, Oh, at present you haven't yet got the courage to write about everything to Vincent, but now we are really and truly brother and sister, and I should be so very happy if you knew me a little too, and, if possible, loved me a little."[48] She felt intimidated by her brother-in-law, and confides to Theo that compared to Vincent, "I feel so small when I think of him—completely insignificant."[49]

Although Vincent, unmoved by Jo's humility, answered her in a condescending, even sarcastic tone, Jo was delighted with his reply. She genuinely admired the works by Vincent that hung on their walls, and writes her sister-in-law, on the subject of *The Starry Night*: ". . . I find it very, very beautiful. How is it, Wil, that of all the paintings that I see at Theo's [at the gallery]—and there are so many that seem bizarre to me—it is always Vincent's that I understand the best and find the prettiest?"[50] Jo was learning more and more about art and architecture from Theo, who relished showing her the capital and taking her to visit artists' studios.

Jo's only concern was looking after Theo's worrisome health; she informed her in-laws that he had finally agreed, after much pleading on her part, to consult Doctor Rivet.

Theo was working very hard, and tells Vincent in detail about what he was organizing and discovering, and that he was always incredibly enthusiastic to receive Vincent's paintings. Theo encourages him: "Some days ago I got your consignment, which is very important; there are superb things in it. Everything arrived in good condition and without any damage. The cradle, the portrait of Roulin, the little sower with the tree, the baby, the starry night, the sunflowers and the chair with the pipe and tobacco pouch are the ones I prefer so far. The first two are very curious. Certainly there is none of the beauty which is taught officially in them, but they have something so striking and so near to truth. . . . Now there is in your canvases a vigor which one certainly does not find in the chromos; in the course of time they will become very beautiful by reason of the settling of the layers of paint and they will undoubtedly be appreciated someday. When we see that the Pissarros, the Gauguins, the Renoirs, the Guillaumins do not sell, one ought to be almost glad of not having the public's favor, seeing that those who have it now will not have it forever, and it is quite possible that times will change very shortly. If you could see how feeble the Salon and the Universal Exhibition are with regard to the pictures, I think you would be of the opinion that they will not last much longer."[51] Theo was right—his talent for farsightedness is evident. Some writers claim that Theo did not recognize Vincent's genius, but by this time there is no doubt about the importance that Theo gave his brother's work. He even asked Vincent for four more canvases to show at the Salon des Indépendants.

Theo writes to him about the challenging aspects of his work: "In all of [your latest paintings] there is a vigor in the colors which you have not achieved before—this in itself constitutes a rare quality—but you have gone further than that, and if there are some who try to find the symbolic by torturing the form, I find this in many of your canvases, namely in the expression of the epitome of your thoughts on nature and living creatures, which you feel to be so strongly inherent in them. But how your brain must have labored, and how you have risked everything to the very limit, where vertigo is inevitable!"[52]

Theo, Vincent's Artistic Advisor

On July 5, 1889, Jo announces to Vincent "a great piece of news, on which we have concentrated a good deal of our attention lately—it is that next winter, toward February probably, we hope to have a baby, a pretty little boy—whom we are going to call Vincent, if you will consent to be his godfather." Vincent was devastated by the news. Just as he seemed to be getting better, this information plunged him back into a depression. Grim memories buried deep in his mind arose with brutal suddenness. The birth of a child represented the end of all his hopes; it signified the final separation from Theo. How could he continue to lavish protection and advice, when he would have to be devoting himself to his child? Vincent would no longer be the first priority for his brother.

Jo's enthusiasm, too, is qualified: "When I told them at Amsterdam and Breda, they all replied, Aren't you pleased, what happiness, etc., etc.—and yet, to tell the honest truth, I was not pleased at all when I found out about it; on the contrary, I was very unhappy, and Theo had a lot of trouble consoling me. It's not that I don't like babies—take my little brother, who is now twelve years old; I held him in my arms when he was hardly two hours old, and I think that there is nothing prettier in the world than a baby—but this is something of a selfish pleasure. When I think how neither Theo nor I are in very good health, I am greatly afraid that we are going to have a weak child, and to my way of thinking the greatest treasure that parents can give to their child is a strong constitution."[53]

Her pregnancy was all the more burdensome because Theo was becoming weaker every day. "I look like a corpse," he writes his brother. Rivet had prescribed several medications, the only positive effect of which was to "put a stop to my cough, which was killing me."[54] It is very likely that Jo was unaware of what exactly her husband was suffering from; at the time, such "hygienic" matters were concealed from a young bride.[55] In early 1888, another doctor had forbidden him "women," and now, two years later, Jo was about to bring his child into the world.

Touched by his sister-in-law's doubts, Vincent writes a charming letter addressed to the couple, arguing that love counts more than anything else, and that the child that is to be born will receive so much love that he could inherit no finer gift from life.[56] He then adds, sadly: "As for being god-father to a son of yours, when to begin with it may be a daughter, honestly, in the circumstances I would rather wait until I am away from here."[57] Nevertheless, the future parents insisted upon their choice, as much out of love for Vincent as to show their gratitude.

As sick as he was, Theo was taking yet another step into adulthood by having a child, as Vincent sank into madness. In early July, when he went out into a high wind to paint a country scene, he was again overwhelmed by an acute attack. He finished his work and returned to the asylum in a pitiful state. At first, Theo was not informed, but a few days later, Vincent's doctor confided to Theo that the situation was very serious. Vincent had never been so gravely stricken. One day, he broke into his studio to eat the paint from the tubes, so that he might both take sustenance and die from his sole passion. The doctor's conclusion was final: painting made Vincent ill, and he would be categorically forbidden to do it until further notice.

Feeling helpless even before this latest dramatic turn of events, Theo sent his brother a brief missive in Dutch, assuring him that nothing had changed between them: "Poor fellow, how dearly I should like to know what to do to put a stop to this nightmare. . . . In your last letter you wrote me that we were brothers for more than one reason. This is what I feel too, and though my heart is not as sensitive as yours, I can enter at times into your feeling of being smothered by so many thoughts that cannot be resolved. Never lose courage, and remember how much I want you."[58]

Vincent implored his brother to intervene and have the prohibition against painting lifted. Before this last crisis, Theo had been lavishing encouragement on him: the Pissarros, Père Tanguy, and others had admired his most recent paintings, including the night scenes and the sunflowers that created "the effect of a piece of cloth embroidered in satin and gold, they're magnificent."[59] Theo had rented space at Père Tanguy's to store Vincent's canvases, which until then had been in his old apartment on Rue Lepic. The new venue would allow them to be seen more easily than at the gallery or at Theo's. The latest and very exciting news came from Brussels, when Octave Maus, the secretary of The XX—The *Vingt*, that is, The Twenty, an artists' collective—contacted Theo about showing some of Vincent's works in their next exhibition.

In 1881, an attorney and celebrated art critic—Octave Maus, with Edmond Picard, had founded the magazine *L'Art moderne* to promote the artistic avant-garde and to boost his country's burgeoning modern painting. From 1883 to 1893, he would direct the secretaryship of the circle of The XX, a group of dynamic artists concerned with the interaction between various artists and art groups in several countries. Intensely interested in the new, he organized attention-getting yearly exhibitions in Brussels—from 1884 to 1886 at the Palais des Beaux-Arts, and from 1887 to 1893 at the Musée Moderne. They featured not only Belgian artists, but foreign guests were also selected every year for their innovative talents. French Impressionists and Post-Impressionists, such as Monet, Pissarro, Seurat, Signac, Toulouse-Lautrec, and even Gauguin—all of whom were first shown at Theo's gallery—had already been invited before Vincent was finally engaged. Maus, an astute critic with a gift for identifying appealing work few were interested in, was a cousin of the painter Eugène Boch, a friend of Vincent.[60] Just like the Indépendants, The XX sought to be an alternative to Brussels's official Salon, where classicism and formulaic academic art were prized. Maus offered the "Vingtistes" the freedom to select and hang their own works.

Theo was overjoyed to be able to announce the news to his brother, but sadly the excited response he expected did not come. Vincent replied that there was no hurry, and that he was not anxious to exhibit because he was dissatisfied with his most recent works. Poor Theo was disappointed, and a bit surprised, but knowing Vincent's mood swings as well as he did, he did not take Vincent's assessment of his work too seriously.

The painter reacted the same way regarding the exhibition of the Indépendants, which opened in September 1889 and to which Theo sent *The Irises* and *Starry Night over the Rhône*. Theo explained: "The latter is hung badly, for one cannot put oneself at a sufficient distance, as the room is very narrow, but the other one makes an extremely good showing."[61] We should remember that the Indépendants were exhibiting in temporary hutments belonging to the Postes et Télégraphes and set up on the ruins of the Tuileries Palace, which had been burned down during the Commune. This salon had neither jury nor prizes, and—theoretically—every type of "audacious" art was allowed.

At this time, Vincent said he wanted to come back

north. The climate of Provence and his isolation no longer suited him. He spoke of the possibility of staying with Pissarro, who often took in painters. Once again, Theo asked him to say clearly what he desired, and encouraged him to come to Paris. Alas, Pissarro's wife was against hosting a "mad painter." Theo tells his brother: "I do not think he has any great authority in his own home, where his wife wears the pants. After a few days he told me that it was not possible in his own house, but that he knows somebody at Auvers who is a doctor and does painting in his spare moments."[62] Pissarro contacted the homeopath Doctor Gachet, "the Impressionists' friend," who was a Socialist and amateur painter, about the possibility of implementing their plan the following spring (fig. 4). In Arles, Doctor Peyron saw no objection.

BESIDES YARDS OF CANVAS, paints, stretchers, and brushes, Theo sent his brother books, reproductions, and newspapers to keep him abreast of Paris events. He constantly encouraged him, passing along the enthusiasm of Isaäcson—one of Vincent's most ardent admirers—about his painting. To supplement his income, Isaäcson wrote criticism on modern art for the Amsterdam weekly *De Portefeuille*. In the August 17, 1889 issue, he prepared a defense that begins: "Who is it who interprets for us, through form and color, that greatness of life, that power of life, of which the 19th century is increasingly aware? I know of one, a solitary pioneer; he struggles alone in the deep night, and his name, Vincent, is destined to go down in the succeeding generations. There will be more to say in time about this remarkable hero—a Dutchman."

At this time, Theo was respecting his brother's wish that his canvases be displayed signed "Vincent," rather than

FIG. 4: VINCENT VAN GOGH, *Dr. Gachet*, 1890.
Sotheby's, New York

"van Gogh." Officially, this was because his last name was unpronounceable in France; unofficially, it was to break the line of descent. No doubt, Vincent also wished to distinguish himself from the other van Gogh—Theo, the Dutch dealer who was so well known in the artistic circles of Paris.

Theo's admiration for Vincent's work was more and more pronounced. In his letters, he began increasingly to take on the posture of a critic. On October 4, 1889: "I like the wheat field and the mountains enormously; they are very beautiful in design. In the wheat field there is that unshakable something which nature has, even in her fiercest aspects. The orchard too is extremely fine."[63] And on October 22: "It seems to me that you are stronger when you paint true things like that [The Irises], or like the stagecoach at Tarascon, or the head of a child, or the underbrush with the ivy in vertical format. The form is so well defined, and the whole is full of color. I understand quite well what it is which preoccupies you in your new canvases, like the village in the moonlight, but I think that the search for some style is prejudicial to the true sentiment of things."[64] And on December 22, 1889: "I received your package containing your wheat field and the two bedrooms. I particularly like the last one, which is like a bouquet of flowers in its coloring. It has a very great intensity of color. The wheat field has perhaps more poetry in it; it is like a memory of something one has once seen. . . . I am curious to see your olive trees; I expect they are beautiful. The sunflowers were on show at Tangui's [sic] this week, and made a very good effect. Your pictures brighten Tangui's shop; Father Tangui is very fond of them, but he does not sell the other things any more than yours."[65] And on January 8, 1890: "As for the other canvases, I very much like the one of those women clambering over the rocks, and the highway with the road menders. I think there is more atmosphere in these last works, more distance than in the preceding ones. Perhaps this is due to your not laying on your paint so thickly everywhere. In one of the rolls there was a superb pen drawing representing a fountain in a garden."[66]

JUST WHEN THINGS SEEMED MORE OR LESS PEACEFUL, Theo learned that another attack had laid Vincent low for several days. At this point, it was unclear if he suffered from epilepsy or had an attack related to his mental illness. The attack occurred at about the time of the birth of Theo's child. Vincent was also worried about his first truly important exhibition. Theo and Maus had taken care of the negotiations and the transportation, and Vincent's canvases arrived in Brussels on January 3, 1890.

After appearing almost uninterested in the invitation initially, Vincent finally decided which paintings to show, and informed Maus: "I accept with pleasure your invitation to show with the XX. This is the list of canvases intended for you: (1) Sunflowers; (2) Sunflowers; (3) Ivy; (4) Orchard in Bloom (Arles); (5) Field of Wheat at Sunrise (Saint-Remy); (6) The Red Vineyard (Montmajour)."[67] He went on to explain that, placed side by side, the paintings would create "a somewhat varied color effect." Cézanne was also invited for the first time that year.

The exhibition opened on January 17. Theo was unable to attend because Jo was so far along in her pregnancy. He relates to his brother on January 22: "It seems that the exhibition of the 'XX' at Brussels is open; I read in a paper that the canvases which arouse the curiosity of the public the most are the open-air study by Cézanne, the landscapes by Sisley, the symphonies by van Gogh and the works of Renoir. . . . I think we can wait patiently for success to come; you will surely live to see it. It is necessary to get well known without obtruding oneself, and it will come of its own accord by reason of your beautiful pictures."[68] On the day before the opening, one of Vincent's paintings created a scandal: the painter Henry De Groux took offense at the fact that his works would be shown next to the "abominable Pot of Sunflowers by Monsieur Vincent or any other agent provocateur."[69] And so the unknown Dutchman was introduced to the art world. Toulouse-Lautrec, rankled to see his friend insulted without the possibility of defending himself, challenged De Groux to a duel, whereupon De Groux was expelled from the group. The duel did not take place.

Albert Aurier first saw Vincent's works in Theo's apartment. In January, he writes in the first issue of the *Mercure de France*, a magazine on literature and the arts: "What makes his entire body of work unique is excess, excess of power, excess of nervousness, and violence in the expression. In his categorical affirmation of the character of things, in his often reckless simplification of forms, in the insolence with which he stares the sun in the face, in his passionate draftsmanship and color, and in the least details of his technique, he shows himself to be powerful, male, one who dares, one who is very brutal and sometimes naïvely delicate."[70] Aurier's long, eloquent article describes beautifully the painter's technique and the force of his expressionistic style. This was the first time an art critic had addressed Vincent's work. Theo, thrilled with the article, sent it to his brother with his compliments.

IN THE MEANTIME, Theo's life was being turned inside out by the birth of his son—another Vincent. On January 31, 1890, he writes an affectionate note asking about his well-being and adds: "[Your relapse] is the only cloud in the sky of our happiness, for, my dear brother, the bad moment for Jo is past. She has brought into the world a beautiful boy, who cries a good deal, but who looks healthy. My poor little wife suffered a lot, because the waters came too soon, but fortunately we had an excellent doctor, who had extraordinary patience, for anyone else in his place would certainly have used forceps. Jo is very well, and has not had any fever, but it might come on yet. The child has started crying already. How happy I should be if after some time, when Jo has recovered, you could come to see her and our little fellow. As we told you at the time, we are going to name him after you, and I devoutly hope that he will be able to be as persevering and as courageous as you."[71]

His birth certificate states that Vincent Willem van Gogh was born on January 31, 1890, at three a.m., at 8, Cité Pigalle. Theo registered him on February 1, at the town hall of the eighteenth arrondissement, in the presence of two witnesses: Andries and Aimé Fouache, a dealer friend of Theo.

After sincere and moving congratulations, Vincent insists: "As for the little boy, why don't you name him Theo, in memory of our Father, that would certainly give me much pleasure."[72] The letter arrived too late; the baby's first name was already entered at the registry office.

The night before she delivered, believing she was dying, Jo opened her heart to Vincent: "So far all has gone well—I must try to be of good heart. Tonight—and all through these days for that matter—I have been wondering so much whether I have really been able to do something to make Theo happy in his marriage—he certainly has me. He has been so good to me, so good—if things should not turn out well—if I should have to leave him—then you must tell him—for there is nobody on earth he loves so much—that he must never regret that he married me, for he has made me, oh, so happy. It is true that such a message sounds sentimental—but I cannot tell him now—for half of my company has fallen asleep, he, too, for he is so very tired."[73]

Wil and Jo's mothers were there to help the soon-to-be mother, while the doctor rested in the next room. When he announced the next morning that the child was born healthy, the family gathered to read Aurier's glowing review of Vincent's work. At last, Jo believed happiness to be at hand (fig. 5).

There was another reason to celebrate. Theo sold one of Vincent's canvases: Anna Boch, a painter and sister of Eugène Boch—both of whom showed at The XX in Brussels—bought *The Red Vineyard* from him for four hundred Belgian francs. Theo generously gave the entire sum to his brother, who announced the milestone to his mother with childlike enthusiasm.

In March, Jo and Theo went to the Salon des Indépendants, where Vincent was exhibiting again. The French president Marie-François Carnot visited during the opening. Theo tells his brother: "A lot of people came to us and asked us to send you their compliments. Gauguin said that your pictures were the chief attraction of the exhibition";[74] and in letters a few days later, he writes, "Pissarro, who went there every day, tells me that you have achieved real success with

FIG. 5: *Johanna van Gogh-Bonger and Vincent Willem van Gogh, c. July 1890*

the artists";[75] and "Monet said that your pictures were the best of all in the exhibition."[76]

Once more, the family considered Vincent's return to Paris or its environs. His friends were worried, because he was yet again weakened by a series of attacks. Theo wrote him a curious letter, both compassionate and obviously happy, that reveals his dilemma—Vincent or Jo? "Your silence proves to us that you are still suffering, and I feel urgently impelled to tell you, my dear brother, that Jo and I suffer too because we know you are ill.... [A]s soon as you feel the need of it, you will say the word, and I shall come at once. Last week it was already a year since I got married. How time flies. We have every reason to be satisfied with this year. I do not forget that you insisted on my getting married, and you were right, for I am much happier. It is true that my dear wife is not like everybody, and that I was marvelously lucky when I found her. We understand each other very well, and our home is pleasant. The little one particularly gives Jo a lot of work, but he is growing surprisingly. He is of a nervous disposition but very [sweet]."[77] And to put the finishing touches on this idyllic picture, Theo adds in his next letter: "If you should want anything, please say so. Business is good, and I have everything I want."[78]

Alas, what Vincent desperately needed, Theo could not give him. Years before, Vincent had exclaimed: "A wife you cannot give me, a child you cannot give me, work you cannot give me. Money, yes—but what good is it to me?"[79] Vincent's situation remained unchanged, while Theo now had all those things.

TO PAVE THE WAY FOR VINCENT'S MOVE TO AUVERS, Theo writes: "I am very happy to be able to tell you that I met Dr. Gachet, that physician Pissarro mentioned to me. He gives the impression of being a man of understanding. Physically he is a little like you. . . . When I told him how your crisis came about, he said to me that he didn't believe it had anything to do with madness, and that if it was what he thought he could guarantee your recovery."[80] Theo hoped to have found a good solution for his brother's future. Vincent could now prepare for his trip.

On the morning of May, 17, 1890, Theo took a hackney cab to meet his brother at the Gare de Lyon. Anxious as he was about the journey his brother had wanted to make alone, Theo had not slept at all. Jo waited impatiently at a window at home. The springtime sunshine warmed the cobblestones of the little dead end. Time passed, and there was no sign of the brothers. Concerned—fearing something went wrong with Vincent—Jo was immediately relieved to finally see them. But what a surprise, too: Vincent looked so much stronger than Theo—who was sickly and stooped from fatigue—so much ruddier than his ashen brother.

When the introductions were over, Theo took Vincent into the baby's room. They bent over the cradle together. Tears welled in their tired eyes. Jo was touched as she watched. Vincent turned to her and urged, "Don't cover him with too much lace, little sister."

For three days they shared the joys of family life, but Vincent, uncomfortable in the bustling city, went to the tiny village of Auvers-sur-Oise earlier than originally planned. Gachet received him in his office, rather than in his clinic in the faubourg Saint-Denis. The doctor would be treating the painter as a friend.

PAUL-FERDINAND GACHET, *Vincent van Gogh on his
Deathbed*, 1890. Van Gogh Museum, Amsterdam

6 A TRAGIC FATE

May 1890–January 1891

Vincent liked Auvers-sur-Oise; it was a pleasant and peaceful place. He was not the first
painter to be charmed by the little village at
the foot of a hill. Daubigny moved there in 1860 and regularly
hosted Daumier and Corot in that tranquil countryside.
Other artists also came, including Renoir, Monet, Pissarro,
and Cézanne, who painted his famous *Hanged Man's House*
there. They all socialized with Gachet, an eccentric figure who
was wildly enthusiastic about art. The people of the village
considered him a character, and the sight of him strolling the
streets with his goat Henriette was very startling. It was into
these hands that Theo had entrusted Vincent's future. "For
now, [Vincent] is entirely well. You would be doing me a great
service if you would be so kind as to take him into your care."[1]
So read the note that Theo wrote and that Vincent gave the
doctor during their first interview.

After auscultating Vincent, Gachet reassured him about his health, and prescribed no medications. The best remedy was not to think about his illness anymore, to paint, and to eat healthy.[2] Despite the differences between them, the two men learned to appreciate each other, especially because they shared a passion for art. Gachet encouraged Vincent, because he was interested in his work. He often invited him over on Sunday for luncheons that seemed too lavish to Vincent, who for years had been content with frugal meals. Vincent very quickly resumed painting; he executed a portrait of the doctor, and one of his daughter, Marguerite, who was then eighteen years old.

Vincent's was a very simple lifestyle, organized around his work. He rose early, painted all day, and took his meals at the Ravouxes' inn, where he lived. While Vincent was regaining a degree of emotional balance, Theo was busy at the gallery, very caught up in organizing an exhibition of the work of the painter Raffaëlli, which would prove to be an unqualified success. The gallery remained open until ten at night.[3] "The Raffaëlli exhibition is attracting a lot of people and we are selling a great deal."[4] Though Theo preferred his show of Pissarro's works, he was very satisfied with this one. Gachet, visiting him at the gallery on June 4, gave him news of Vincent, declaring that his brother's health was much better, and that he believed him to be completely cured. Theo, realizing his difficulties were dissipating, was relieved. As the doctor was leaving, he invited Theo, his wife, and little Vincent to lunch with him on the following Sunday.[5]

On June 8, as agreed, the family got off the train at the Chaponval station, where Vincent was waiting for them. He was beaming, genuinely glad to see them again. As a present, he gave his godson a bird's nest, a symbol of a home. The day promised to be magnificent. All together, beneath the trees, they lunched at Gachet's home in an atmosphere of good humor and genuine happiness. A delightful and relaxed feeling permeated that sunny Sunday—a carefree day such as the van Goghs had not experienced in years. Vincent showered his nephew with attention. He wanted to show him the animals that ran free in the garden and laughed when his little namesake was frightened by the crow of a rooster. The painter was full of plans, speaking in particular of his desire to have another exhibition at a Paris café.

After lunch, the van Goghs strolled in the surrounding countryside. The brothers talked about everything, including possible future vacations in Auvers. Although Theo dreamed of coming to the village for a rest—as Vincent had been pressing him to in his letters for some time[6]—he also had to visit his and his wife's families in Holland. For the time being, it was only an idea, because Theo would have had to take three weeks' vacation, and it was not at all certain that he would have been able to. In her memoirs, Adeline Carrié, the innkeepers' daughter, recounts that she first met Theo on July 28, 1890,[7] but it is impossible to imagine that Theo would not have gone to the inn that day, June 8, if only to see his brother's new works—some fifteen paintings, since his arrival on May 20—which Vincent kept in his monkish garret and in the tavern's inner room. At that time, the brothers discussed the possibility of renting a small house and realizing his dream of creating an artists' community.

That country Sunday was a moment of happiness for both of them. Theo, rejoicing to see his brother recovered and in full creative ferment, promised to return soon. Annie Bonger writes her in-laws: "Net [Johanna] and Theo went to

Auvers, where they found Vincent in excellent form. On that count, Theo was freed for the moment of a great worry."[8]

WHILE THEO'S CONCERN FOR HIS BROTHER had eased, a new worry arose: little Vincent fell suddenly ill. "After a restless night," Theo writes his mother and Wil, "he [the baby] fell asleep about nine and awoke at eleven, when the doctor was visiting us. He [the doctor] told us, 'You will not lose your child to this health problem.' Today, he was better."[9]

The child's condition probably resulted from contaminated milk. Eventually, little Vincent recovered. Theo was tormented by the idea that his child might have inherited the ill health of the van Goghs. Still shaken by the last few painful days, he took pen in hand and wrote Vincent a long, heartrending letter. Although his son was securely on the road to recovery, Theo confides to his brother that the experience has marked him deeply: ". . . you never heard anything so grievously distressing as this almost continuous plaintive crying all through many days and many nights, when you don't know what to do, and all you do seems to aggravate his sufferings."[10]

The obvious improvement in Vincent's health led Theo to hope he might be a source of support; in his letter, Theo reveals his many concerns, in an exalted, excessive style that we find in none of his other letters. Curiously, the tone of this letter resembles Vincent's letters in their intensity. His constant health problems, coupled with his worries about the baby's illness, seem to account for this unusual outpouring.[11] He wrote about all his conflicts with his employers, after keeping them from Vincent in order to spare him, and complained of the manner in which Boussod and Valadon treated him. He still suffered from the lack of respect with which they treated him, as if they still considered him a novice in the business. He rails against the meager salary he is receiving, at a time when he needs more money. His exasperation clear, he elaborates once again about his longtime dream of handing in his notice, going out on his own, and finally opening his gallery. How did this frugal lifestyle serve him? "While writing I think I came to the conclusion that this is my duty, and that if Mother, or Jo, or you or I myself should resign ourselves to starvation, it won't be of the slightest service to us—on the contrary. What would be the good of you and me going through the world like a pair of down-and-out beggars with nothing to eat? On the contrary, by keeping up our courage, and by living, all of us, sustained by our mutual love and mutual esteem, we shall make better headway, and we shall be able to fulfill our duty and our task with much greater security than if we were to weigh every mouthful of bread."[12]

He goes on to evoke poetically the landscapes of their childhood, associating them with happy memories: "We shall draw the plow until our strength forsakes us, and we shall still look with admiration at the sun or the moon, according to the hour. We like this better than being put into an armchair and rubbing our legs like the old merchant at Auvers. Look here, old boy, watch your health as much as you can, and I shall do the same, for we have too much in our noodles to forget the daisies and the lumps of earth freshly cast up by the plough, neither do we forget the branches of the shrubs which put forth buds in spring, or the bare branches of the trees shivering in winter, nor the limpid blue of the serene skies, nor the big clouds of autumn, nor the uniformly gray sky in winter, nor the sun rising over our aunts' garden, nor the red sun going down into the sea at Scheveningen, nor the moon and stars of a fine night in summer or winter—no, come what may, this is our profession."[13] We can sense here a man who is tired of fighting, increasingly weakened by the illness eating away at him. A man so weary of this life that the only solution is to leave it all behind and start fresh someplace else. His only salvation is his wife: "As for you, you have found your way, old fellow, your carriage is steady on its wheels and strong, and I am seeing my way, thanks to my dear wife."

He also asks Vincent to calm down: "Take it easy, you, and hold your horses a little, so that there may be no accident, and as for me, an occasional lash of the whip would do me no harm." In those passages, he stresses that Vincent must stop torturing himself. The important thing is to stay healthy and keep painting glorious paintings. Meanwhile, Theo's health had been failing for years.

After so many years, their roles seemed to be reversed: for the length of the letter, Theo was once again the younger brother he should always have been—and that he had been until he took Vincent's fate into his hands.

It was to his elder brother that he addressed questions about subjects as various as vacations, moving into a larger apartment, and, of course, whether he should leave the house of Goupil. And it was of his elder brother that he asked advice about the direction he should take: "What do you have to say to this, old fellow?" Vincent, of course, empathized with the vicissitudes his brother was experiencing. He, too, worried about his godson; he supported Theo in his struggles with his employers and told him he wanted to go see him. Then, he suddenly changed his mind, overcome by an incapacitating feeling of helplessness. His presence, he felt, might be an imposition on his brother and his wife.[14] Vincent considered himself more of a burden than an effective source of support, and felt guilty about being one of Theo's responsibilities. The tenor of his brother's letter destabilized him—although he was on the road to recovery, he was not as well as Theo believed.

The weeks he had spent in Auvers had allowed him to regain some inner tranquility; nevertheless, Theo's missive brought everything to the fore. If for some reason Theo could no longer maintain him, Vincent would have to stop his own work. What reply could Vincent give—he who lived solely on the allowance his brother gave him—when Theo asked his advice on his professional situation? Naturally, he understood his brother's distress, but an answer did not come easily. Vincent remained evasive: "That will be as it may, you have not spared yourself trouble for them, you have served them with exemplary loyalty at all times."[15] Long gone were the days when Vincent pleaded with Theo to leave everything and come join him in Drenthe and become a painter. Now, what he feared was that Theo would decide to quit the gallery. "Was he [Vincent] aware," G. Kraus writes "that his psychiatrist was becoming his patient. . . . The material and spiritual aspects of their symbiosis were more at risk than ever before."[16] The foundations of the Theo–Vincent pair were about to be undermined.

IN A LETTER DATED JULY 5, Theo—given the impossibility of going to Auvers because of his work and family life—again suggests that Vincent come to Paris.[17] Now that his son had recovered, Theo saw no reason not to invite his brother for a Sunday visit. He even proposed a schedule: a visit to Tanguy's to meet Walpole Brook, a painter who had met Vincent in Auvers and who wanted to see his paintings; a trip to a second-hand shop to admire a Japanese Buddha, and, of course, lunch at chez van Gogh.

On Sunday, July 6, Vincent—who had not been back in Paris since leaving for Auvers—arrived in the capital by the first morning train. The early part of the day went as planned. At Tanguy's, Vincent objected when he saw where his canvases were kept—a "bedbug infested hole."[18] Next, they went together to the secondhand shop, then Vincent probably saw Toulouse-Lautrec at the latter's studio on Rue Caulaincourt. There, he admired the painting *Mademoiselle Dihau at the Piano*, which Theo had noticed at the Salon des Indépendants. Lautrec, who was also invited for lunch, went back to the van Goghs' with Theo and Vincent. In honor of his brother's visit, Theo had invited a few friends, in particular, the art critic Albert Aurier, author of the remarkable article praising Vincent's work earlier that year.

Vincent enjoyed all these various interactions, yet, disturbed and worried, decided to go back to Auvers that same night, without waiting for his friend Guillaumin. Since he had been invited to spend several days in Paris, his early departure indicated something was wrong.

It is true that the Paris apartment was infused with a tension so extreme that not even Toulouse-Lautrec's legendary good humor could ease it. Theo and Jo confessed to being exhausted, physically and psychically worn-out by their son's recent illness. The difficult time with their son rendered them less available, more irritable, and less open to Vincent. Theo looked unwell: his persistent health problems were writ large on his face.

A few incidents marked the day: first, there was an animated discussion between the Bongers and the van Goghs about the building's ground-floor apartment. Theo would have liked his brother-in-law to move in, but his wife Annie was reluctant. She did not get along with the van Goghs, and had a curious fear that she would have to act as their maid.[19] Then Jo and Vincent disagreed about how to hang a painting by Benoît Louis Prevost.[20] Vincent was also critical about the lack of space available to show his paintings in his brother's home. Once again, the subject of moving to a larger apartment arose. Larger, and therefore more expensive. And this was no time to be increasing expenses. Nevertheless, in his letter of July 5, Theo seems more optimistic, confident, and serene, as if his fears have miraculously dissolved. He emphasizes his success in business—important sales for the gallery—and is exhilarated because he sold two canvases by Gauguin.[21]

The reality was just the opposite. After Theo's desperate missive of June 30, he was undoubtedly aware of the ongoing need to manage his brother, who was still so fragile and high-strung. In his most recent communication, therefore, he downplays the situation, and in so doing partly conceals the truth. In reality, nothing positive had emerged with respect to his employers. He was consumed by the continuing dilemma of whether to remain with the house of Goupil or go. This thorny subject fueled most of the conversation after the guests left, along with the endlessly recurring question of money. Theo was finding it more and more difficult to make ends meet with what he earned. The only solution, if he was to provide decently for his household, his brother, and the other members of his family, was to get a raise, which his employers consistently refused him.

The situation set off a violent argument between husband and wife. Jo argued vehemently against Theo's leaving the gallery. Driven by anger, might she have criticized her brother-in-law, insinuating, for example, that he was too much of a burden for Theo to bear? They disagreed on what was to be done. The tension between them affected Vincent deeply, and as he left Paris, he could not envision his future. His brother had not told him clearly whether or not he would still receive his usual 150 francs a month.

Without that money, Vincent would no longer be able to dedicate himself to his work.[22] Jo, feeling guilty, answered Vincent's anguished letters. In correspondence that has not been preserved, she comforts and reassures him about his future and their future together.

That Sunday, July 6, represented the beginning of a new phase in the relationship between the two brothers. A rift was forming between them—the preoccupations that Theo was handling as best he could were overwhelming Vincent. It was obvious to him that a lack of money and other difficulties were eating away at Theo. Their lives all depended on him—on Theo, a fragile, sickly man.

DURING THAT SUNDAY, Theo and Jo told Vincent of their plans to spend the summer holidays in Holland; they wanted their respective families to meet their six-month-old baby. The idea of going to Auvers for a few days was set aside. Vincent was immensely disappointed. He had been looking forward to their being together in that healthy, tranquil countryside, far from the capital's frenzied pace. Now he felt abandoned, even betrayed, by the person closest to him.

He pressed Theo and Jo to reconsider. Clumsily, he pointed out what the expenses of such a trip could amount to, and emphasized how the region's health-giving air would completely restore their son.

It was no use; Theo did not change his mind. Because

Jo felt weak, he hoped that she would recuperate quickly within the circle of her affectionate family, but the trip was no vacation for Theo, who would accompany his wife and child, and take advantage of the time to attend to business matters. Before leaving for Holland, he lets Vincent know some of what is happening, in an attempt to reassure him and minimize some of the issues that are still unresolved: "The danger is really not as great as you thought."[23] He stresses that the most important thing in life is to be healthy. But he says nothing specific about his money problems, leaving Vincent uncertain as to what is happening. After all, Theo, too, was in a state of uncertainty. He had gathered the courage to face Boussod and Valadon to explain why he needed a raise. On July 7, he had even given them an ultimatum—if his employers refused his conditions, he would resign. And all he received in return was their silence. He writes Vincent: "Although the eight days are past now, those gentlemen have not said a word about what they intend to do with me," and enclosed a fifty-franc note. [24]

He was unaware that he was leaving behind him in Auvers a brother in torment, who was losing his equilibrium, struggling against his demons, and painting frantically to exhaustion. In particular, Vincent executed two great works: *Field under a Stormy Sky* and *Wheat Field with Crows*.

On July 15, Theo left for Holland without meeting with Monet, along with Valadon, as agreed; the painter had delayed their appointment until the following month. Theo stopped off for a brief visit with his family, now living in Leiden; seeing his mother and Wil again, even for a short time, made him very happy. Anna melted at the sight of her grandson.

His schedule was very full for someone as tired and sick as he was. In the end, he did not go to The Hague to see the painter Hendrik Willem Mesdag, who had just bought a canvas by Corot, *Streams in the Dunes.* On Thursday, July 17, Theo, leaving his wife and child, departed Leiden for Antwerp, where he met with Emile Clarembaux, a Brussels art dealer, to see about some business matters, including finding a buyer for a painting by Narcisse Virgile Diaz de la Peña.[25]

That evening, Theo and Clarembaux returned, exhausted, to Brussels, without having closed the smallest sale. The next day, Theo sent Jo a letter from the Hotel Mengelle, relating everything that happened since they parted. He writes, sadly, "I kept thinking of you [Jo and little Vincent] all the time. I can't get used to not seeing you."[26] The negotiations over the Diaz having failed, he moved up his return to Paris, originally planned for July 20. Theo was once more plunged, as he put it, back into the "Paris bazaar" on July 19.

Alone in Paris

THIS WAS THE fIRST TIME since getting married that Theo and Jo had been apart. In their correspondence, they sound like young lovers. They sent each other little notes almost every day, covering each other with hundreds of kisses. *"Dearest husband of mine, how pleased I shall be to see you again—are you coming soon? Never again will I leave you — never, ever again."* She adds: "Don't laugh at me, but I've just come to realise how sacrosanct and inviolable marriage is—how deeply attached one becomes. Oh, how I miss you."[27]

Alone in Paris, Theo was upset about being in an empty apartment that seemed cold and soulless, because he so desperately missed the warm presence of his wife and child: "Yes, dearest, I miss you too, and I picture you and the little one before me a hundred times a day. It's true that you only appreciate one another fully when you're separated & realize that love can be indestructible."[28] And later on, after Jo teases him about "regaining his freedom," Theo replies bluntly: "What do you take me for! I am so flustered & don't feel I belong anywhere, so I'm all too aware of your absence and would be, even without this powerful feeling, which doesn't deceive me."[29]

Naturally, their child's health was their central preoccupation. Jo described little Vincent's behavior in great detail, reassuring her husband by telling him how the baby was getting stronger and healthier. There was nothing to fear on that account, as the worst was behind them. Theo's mind was at ease on this issue, at least. But his professional situation was still uncertain—there was no word from his employers.

Once back in Paris, he went to the firm's headquarters on Rue Chaptal, where he found the Boussods, father and son, chatting about the art business in front of some canvases. As neither one broached the subject that was on his mind, Theo, despite his fear, took the initiative, explaining to Etienne Boussod that after considerable reflection he wished to remain with the firm under any conditions. He added: "I told Mr. Etienne that . . . I had changed my mind & if he couldn't increase my remuneration I would see what economies I could make to get by, and that for my family's sake I'd prefer not to venture anything for the time being."[30] His employer replied that he saw no objection. Theo was a discerning art dealer, an excellent asset; it was a stroke of good luck to keep him on at the gallery without a raise. Yet, Etienne Boussod, to demonstrate his understanding, said: "[O]h, mais ne vous inquiétez pas, nous verrons [Don't worry, we shall see]."[31]

Theo's relief following this conversation is evident in his letters. In Holland, he had been tormented by the idea of leaving everything behind. He admits as much to his mother: "Now that I am back here, it is clear that it was too risky to leave my trade, my position, to go toward the unknown. That is too dangerous. . . . I was desperate to see that things had gotten to that point. . . ."[32] Theo would never achieve his dream.

Ever since he had moved to Paris, he had been assigned the role of the family provider, which he accepted and bore, with all its consequences. Aware of that reality, he writes: "[M]uch as I would like to be independent, I shall refrain from pursuing this now. We'll just have to wait for a more favorable opportunity to present itself."[33] The idea that he would no longer be able to meet the needs of his immediate family, nor to help his family abroad could not but paralyze his decisions. In the same letter he lets her know about his discussion with his employers.[34] He told her that he would not be resigning his position. Ever cautious, he stated that nothing was really definite or certain. "They've done such good business at Rue Chaptal, mainly with Chauchard, that it seems to have gone to their heads. They're talking about closing down the retail branches and doing everything from Rue Chaptal. It's enough to drive one out of one's mind. But it's important to be cautious, that's certain. . . ."[35] Thus, the idea of moving to a larger apartment seemed at a standstill. Jo showed sympathy and solicitude: "Oh, my love, I'm sorry you're brooding so over tiresome money matters. . . . I think you're absolutely right about moving—our little apartment is far too pleasant and cozy for us to go rushing out of it, and it would certainly be wiser to keep our expenses as low as possible. I shall honestly do my best as well."[36] Despite all the recent difficulties, Jo and Theo remained very close, allies in adversity. They would face any obstacles together: "I will do my utmost not to be a burden but to help you."[37]

In Paris, Theo was again steeped in the tension he so disliked. He worked like a madman at the gallery, hoping to do good business, if only to impress his employers. Impressive sales might cause them to reconsider their position with respect to a possible raise. He even made another trip to Brussels and back on July 23 about the Diaz. His letters to Jo permit us to establish what he did and when: with his wife away, and to avoid the loneliness that weighed upon him, he often went out at night, rediscovering the warmth of the Montmartre he loved. As he used to, he dined at Mère Bataille's. He saw Dries and Annie regularly, for lunch or for a picnic in the Meudon forest. Their disagreements about the apartment had evaporated. Theo knew his best friend's chilliness, and that he often deferred to his wife's decisions, and he accepted it: "[H]e is like that and there is no reason to break with him."[38]

Theo, seeking warmth and friendship, often went to Vésinet, to the home of M. Francken, a banker and collector, and his uncle Cor's brother-in-law. His social life was very full: lunch with Manzi, a typographer who worked for Boussod and Valadon, or the theater with Velten, an architect related to Hans Velten, who worked for the London print sellers Obach and Co. He tried to distract himself from the loneliness by keeping busy, impatiently waiting until he could be with his wife again. He dreamed of resting beside her and his son, making plans, and getting some of his strength back. He had no inkling of the dreadful news that was about to turn his life inside out.

Vincent's Death

O N MONDAY, JULY 28, at about nine thirty in the morning, Theo was amazed to see the Dutch painter Anton Hirschig enter his gallery. Hirschig, charged with looking after Theo's brother in Auvers, lived at the Ravoux tavern, in a room adjacent to Vincent's. Hirschig brought a letter from Gachet urging Theo to come quickly: It said that Vincent was in danger! Theo, terribly worried, left immediately. When he entered Vincent's tiny, austere room, he was stricken by the terrifying sight of his wounded brother. Vincent had shot himself in the chest the day before; now, he was dying. The unbearable sight caused Theo to burst into floods of tears. Very calmly, Vincent tried to comfort him: "Don't cry, I did it for everyone's good. . . ." An extreme act to save Theo and his family, a proof of love, perhaps. But certainly the gesture of a desperate man. The two men spoke for a long while, in Dutch.

Seeing Theo, Vincent seemed to regain his strength somewhat, and this could explain Theo's reassuring words in the letter that he immediately wrote Jo: "[I] found him better than I had expected, although he is indeed very ill. . . . If he's better tonight, I'll go back to Paris early tomorrow morning, but if not, I shall stay on here. . . . Don't worry too much. It was just as desperate before, and the physicians were surprised by his strong constitution."[39] He wanted to save him, as he had done all his life, but Vincent was done with struggling. He sank into unconsciousness, then woke for a few moments, just long enough to murmur that that was how he wished to die.[40] On the night of July 29, at one thirty, Vincent died in Theo's arms.

THEO STAYED WITH VINCENT'S BODY UNTIL MORNING. Despite being in a state of shock, he had to deal with administrative details and take care of the burial arrangements: registering the death; choosing the casket; purchasing a fifteen-year grave grant for thirty francs; and wrangling with Father Tessier, who refused to lend a hearse because he believed a suicide was no longer the responsibility of a Christian community. In the end, the mayor of Méry-sur-Oise put the commune's vehicle at Theo's disposal. In his immense sorrow, he set himself to putting Vincent's affairs in order. It was then that he noticed an unfinished letter from his brother—apparently a reply to one of his own, which has not survived—in which Vincent praised Theo's courage: "Well, the truth is, we can only make our pictures speak. But still, my dear brother, there is this that I have always told you, and I repeat it once more with all the earnestness that can be imparted by an effort of a mind diligently fixed on trying to do as well as one can—I tell you again that I shall always consider that you are something other than a simple dealer in Corots, that through my mediation you have your part in the actual production of some canvases, which even in the cataclysm retain their quietude. . . . I have risked my life for my work. . . . "[41] It was a letter that tolled like a farewell.

On Wednesday, July 30, 1890, at about three o'clock in the afternoon, a funeral procession left the Ravoux tavern and made its way toward the little cemetery overlooking Auvers-sur-Oise. At the head of the procession, Theo wept for his brother, dead at the age of thirty-seven. His brother-in-law and friend, Andries, held him as they walked. Behind Theo followed Doctor Gachet and his son, Paul; artists who were close friends, such as Lucien Pissarro, Emile Bernard, Gauguin's companion in Martinique, Charles Laval, and Père

Tanguy; and those who were with Vincent at the end of his life, such as Ravoux and Hirschig. Vincent's faithful friend Camille Pissarro, detained in Eragny, sent a moving condolence letter: "This morning, we received the mournful news of your poor brother's death. My son, Lucien, had only a few minutes to catch the train. . . . I would very much have wanted to do so, too, but I could not get ready in time. I greatly regret it, because I was really very fond of that artist's soul that was your brother, and who will leave a great void among the young."[42] Emile Bernard described the burial to the critic Albert Aurier with great sensitivity: "The sun was terribly hot outside. We climbed the hill outside Auvers talking about him, about the daring impulse he had given to art, of the great projects he was always thinking about, and of the good he had done to all of us. We reached the cemetery, a small new cemetery strewn with new tombstones. It is on the little hill above the fields that were ripe for harvest under the wide blue sky that he would still have loved . . . perhaps. Then he was lowered into the grave. . . . Anyone would have started crying at that moment . . . the day was too much made for him for one not to imagine that he was still alive and enjoying it. . . ."[43] At Vincent's grave, which was crowned by a small stone designed by Theo and Gachet, Gachet ended the civil ceremony with a brief and laudatory speech. Too much in the throes of his overwhelming grief, Theo could not speak, though he was able to sincerely thank those who had come to pay Vincent their last respects. He was very shaken as he left his beloved brother and a huge part of his life behind forever, in "a sunny spot among the wheatfields."[44] And indeed he would never again have the opportunity to meditate by his grave.

Back in Vincent's room, which was brightened by his most recent paintings and many bouquets, Theo gave some of his brother's works to the people who were around him in the last days of his life, as a token of gratitude. Levert, the carpenter who made his coffin; the Ravouxes, who kept the inn; and Doctor Gachet were the principal beneficiaries. Devastated by the experience, Theo was only a shadow of himself. He could not bear to remain in the village, which was so painfully associated with the loss of his brother. He decided to leave for Paris that very evening and accepted Annie and Andries's invitation to spend the night with them. He needed to have people around him: "I managed to leave in the evening, but oh, how empty it is everywhere. I miss him so; everything seems to remind me of him."[45]

Had Theo really not foreseen the possibility of such a tragedy? In that summer of 1890, he was worried, even tormented about what would become of Vincent, but no more intensely so than during the period of the attacks in Arles and Saint-Rémy. He was perfectly aware of his brother's extreme behavior, and his violent, impulsive reactions. He had learned over time to soothe them, defuse them, either with words of reassurance or with peremptory suggestions. For Theo, immediate danger meant the onset of the next attack—not the final act of suicide. And yet, he had noticed a withdrawal immediately before, and tried to address this with his brother: "[S]ince you say that you write with difficulty, and don't talk about your work I am a little afraid that there is something troubling you or not going right."[46] In critical moments such as these, he advised Vincent to consult Doctor Gachet, believing that he was the only one who could help.

Theo's last letter to Vincent, which was a reply to one of Vincent's letters, reveals the painter's relentless difficulties.[47] Apparently, Vincent had once again brought up the events of that July 6, which continued to haunt him. Jo, consumed by remorse, writes: "Did we go too far the day he came? My dearest, I have firmly resolved never to squabble with you again—and always to do what you wish."[48]

When she learned of Vincent's death, Jo clearly felt guilty for upsetting him. She understood how fragile Vincent was: "Oh, how I should have liked to see him again and say how sorry I was for having been impatient with him the last time."[49]

What were the triggers for Vincent's suicide? G. Kraus explains his suicide as the result of a conjunction of three factors: the lack of money, which was becoming critical; Theo's marriage to Jo (and its natural consequence, their son, Vincent); and Theo's illness, whose visible progression had made a profound impression on Vincent.[50]

Still, one mystery remains to be explained: why did Theo not mention in his letter to his brother of July 22 his decision not to leave the house of Goupil? Vincent's reply to that letter proves this omission, as he tells Theo he hopes that "the Gentlemen will be well disposed toward you."[51] Had Theo given Vincent that information, he might have altered the course of events. Would Vincent have committed suicide anyway, if he had known that his brother was keeping his position? No one can say. He was in such torment, so weary of his life: "It is a grief that will weigh on me for a long time and will certainly not leave my thoughts as long as I live, but if one should want to say anything about it, it is that he himself has found the rest he so much longed for,"[52] Theo writes his mother.

THEO WAS SURROUNDED BY FRIENDS and acquaintances, but faced with this intolerable tragedy, he wanted to be with his family. Only they could provide consolation and support, and ease the emptiness that Vincent had left behind. Theo had expressed this feeling to his wife upon arriving in Auvers: "Rest assured that I will manage, no matter what may happen, after all, I have you to live for; I'll not be alone as long as I have my wife & my little boy."[53]

He sent his beloved mother a very touching letter, in which he says he hopes to see her again soon in this moment that is so sorrowful for the whole family.[54] He decided to leave for Leiden on August 3. Together, Anna and Theo evoked memories of Vincent telling each other anecdotes about him, little details that mitigated their anguish. Rereading his letters, they rediscovered the passionate, extraordinary person they missed so much.[55] At the family reunion, Theo opened the subject of what was to become of Vincent's paintings. He proposed to his three sisters and to Joan van Houten, Anna's husband, that they sign a letter stating that Theo was his elder brother's sole heir.[56] This was intended to protect his works, which would one day be appreciated and therefore increase in value. The signatories of this document accepted the terms of this arrangement without demur. It is true that most of the family did not believe in Vincent's talent, especially Anna, who had never accepted the fact that everyone in the family had made sacrifices for him. On August 9, Theo went to Amsterdam, to the Bongers, with Jo and his son. A few days after arriving, he wrote to his mother and Wil. Still replaying the events leading to Vincent's suicide, he writes: ". . . And, when he went to bed, evidently everything that had gone on recently came to the surface."[57]

Despite his grief, Theo had to face the professional responsibilities that awaited him in Paris. He returned around August 17, and got back to work immediately, albeit halfheartedly. He would dedicate what energy he had left, not to selling paintings in the gallery, but to seeing that his brother's talent was recognized. He was driven by a single obsession: to exhibit Vincent's works. He was determined to succeed at last in the mission he had been unable to realize while his brother was alive: to help his genius be recognized. "I hope it can be done, because to let these masterly canvases remain unknown would be unpardonable on my part, and if I did not do everything I could right away to try to make that happen, I could never forgive myself."[58] Theo finally replied to the many expressions of condolence he received after Vincent's funeral, including those from Claude Monet, Meijer de Haan, Camille Pissarro, John Russell, Armand Guillaumin, and Albert Aurier. Paul Gauguin also sent a note, though it seemed a little distant given their once close friendship. All these gestures of sympathy comforted him and reminded him that his peers recognized Vincent as a great artist.

Theo, soon after returning to Paris, went in search of somewhere to show his brother's canvases. The gallery he managed was out of the question, due to the stormy relations between himself and Boussod and Valadon. They would never have agreed to show the works of an unknown, eccentric painter who was the brother of one of their employees. They would not jeopardize their reputation. Theo turned to the art dealer Paul Durand-Ruel—Boussod and Valadon's competitor—who had always promoted avant-garde art. Theo invited him to his home to see the paintings he kept there. "Durand-Ruel . . . stayed more than an hour and then had to leave, for he has not yet seen one of his works from Auvers since those are at Tanguy's. What he saw he found very artistic and very remarkable, but he is still hesitating about an exhibition in his gallery as he is afraid that it will start a controversy. He suggested himself if I could receive him again next week. . . ."[59] Trying to get someone to exhibit

Vincent's work was going to be difficult, because of the dealers' icy response to the new. Theo met Durand-Ruel's son, who told him that his father was thinking of making a room available to him that winter, but nothing seemed to be definite. Theo considered other venues in Paris. Signac suggested a separate room in a pavilion belonging to the city, during the Salon des Indépendants.[60]

In addition to his plan for an exhibition, Theo writes in a letter to Aurier of his idea of publishing a biography of Vincent: "You were the first to appreciate him, not only for his more or less great talent for painting pictures, but you have also understood his works and have seen in them exactly the man he was. Several writers have expressed the desire to write something about him, but I have asked them to wait because I wanted to be the first to give you the chance to be the first to speak and, if you wish, to write a biography for which I would furnish you all the material which is altogether authentic as I have had a very steady correspondence with him since 1873 and have numerous other interesting documents."[61] Touched and honored by the request, Aurier was quick to accept. However, the publication of his forthcoming novel prevented him from starting on it, and Aurier's premature death put an end to the project. Theo did find an outlet—the magazine *Art et Critique*—for the article on Vincent that Gachet was working on.[62]

The van Goghs' apartment became the scene of an unusual degree of activity. Theo had many visitors, and all these visits revolved around one central point: Vincent. Camille Pissarro, taking advantage of a trip to Paris, went to Theo's. Fascinated by his last paintings, he wished to trade for one of his. The painter and lithographer Serret also went to see Vincent's works: "[Serret] asked me a lot of questions about

[Pa and Moe] to find out where he got such masterly talent and genius from."[63] All these expressions of admiration encouraged Theo to continue to pursue his goal. A visit from Gachet provided another opportunity to share memories of the deceased. "Dr. Gachet brought me a sketch in pencil after a portrait of Vincent, which he had made as an exercise for the etching he wanted to make later on, as well as a small drawing of a sunflower."[64] During this same period, Theo contacted Octave Maus to organize a retrospective of his brother's works in the context of the 1891 exhibition of The XX.[65] All these plans palliated his anguish as he continued to think about his brother's death. Deeply touched by the solicitude of these various people, he was immensely grateful to them for their support of him and his brother's work.

If a handful of artists and dealers recognized Vincent's talent, the wider art world was far from sharing their enthusiasm. Even Durand-Ruel, as unintimidated as he was in the face of challenging art, in the end refused to show Vincent's paintings, ostensibly because the general public was sure to find them objectionable.[66] Theo persevered and did not become discouraged. Knowing Emile Bernard's admiration for Vincent's work, Theo appealed to him, hoping the painter would be willing to help him arrange Vincent's paintings throughout the new apartment that Theo had finally decided to rent in the same building on the second floor: "[T]he number of his canvases is staggering. I can't cope with them in assembling a group which would give an idea of his work."[67] This way, in the absence of an exhibition, he could at least show Vincent's work. Emile Bernard accepted and went to Theo's to help. Theo was proud of the result. He writes to Wil: "He [Emile Bernard] did a good job of hanging everything. . . . He also painted a shepherd and sheep on our living-room windows. It looks like medieval stained glass. It goes very well with the room, which is decorated with Vincent's paintings. I wish you could see it. You would get something out of it, and you would see that, unlike what that Monsieur Beaubourg said in his article, these canvases are not the work of a sick mind, but of the ardor and humanity of a great man."[68] Theo's apartment became a museum dedicated to Vincent's memory.

During this time, he mentions his work at the gallery very little in his letters. We learn only that he closed an important sale, a painting by Constant Troyon, a landscape painter of the Barbizon School. A considerable achievement, considering the profits the transaction brought in: ". . . 10,000 francs—and the promise of more business."[69] In addition, two letters to Camille Pissarro underscore the sale to a collector, Dupuis, of one of his paintings, *Field with the Laborer*, for eight hundred francs and Theo's desire to organize another exhibition, given this news and the painter's magnificent recent production.[70] Through these two letters, it seems that Theo had not lost his will to tirelessly champion the Impressionists, and the proof of this was his desire to exhibit work by his friend Pissarro. He also succeeded in selling a Guillaumin and a Degas. But Vincent remained his priority. Come what may, he was determined to achieve posthumous recognition for Vincent. He set out on a frantic race, a struggle against the clock, as if every minute counted. And indeed it did.

EVER SINCE HIS RETURN TO PARIS, Theo seemed to have regained his physical strength. ". . . I am getting better too. Every day I take the drops that Dr. Van der Maaten [a writer, doctor, and friend of the family] has prescribed; I sleep better and the coughing has almost stopped."[71] Dries Bonger, for his part, reassures his family about his brother-in-law's health: "He is better. He was very depressed. Vincent's death affected him terribly."[72] Unfortunately, the remission was short-lived. The disease that had been consuming Theo for years suddenly flared up, becoming acute in September and October. He writes Doctor Gachet: ". . . [M]y health is far from good; I have the feeling that my head is spinning and whatever I write gives me the feeling of dizziness. It's again the nerves that have got the upper hand."[73] He relates his sufferings to his mother in detail: "I had become so sick by the drops of that Dr. that I would have become insane. They helped stun me during the night and prevented me from coughing, but they gave me hallucinations and nightmares night and day to the extent that I would have jumped out of the window or would have killed myself in one way or another if I should not have stopped taking them. . . . When I stopped with them the coughing came back with a vengeance, and this led to a heavy cold and hoarseness. . . . Dr. Leon Simon (whom I had consulted at the advice and with an introduction from Dr. Gatchet) told me, 'If you would stay home it would be good for your coughing, but your nervousness would come back.' No need to tell you that I listened to him,"[74] Theo's health became very worrisome. On October 4, Jo's birthday, he was in a state of extreme agitation. A short time later, the tragedy exploded; Camille Pissarro reports: "It seems that van Gogh was ill before his madness, he had a retention of urine; eight days already he did not urinate; apart from that there were his worries, his sorrows, and a violent discussion with his employers about a painting by Decamps. As a result he has, in a moment of exasperation, taken his leave from the Boussods, and all at once he has become mad, he wanted to rent the Tambourin in order to found an association of painters. He then became violent; he who loved his wife and son so dearly, he wanted to kill them."[75] His behavior was entirely at odds with his real personality. His inconsolable sorrow and the tension that had been building since Vincent's death—undoubtedly aggravated by his illness—set off the attack of insanity. Other symptoms would unfortunately be revealed.

It was during this crisis that Theo sent Gauguin his famous message: "Departure to tropics assured, money follows—Theo, Director"[76] Gauguin had no reason not to believe him. On the one hand, he was well aware of his dealer's honesty, and on the other, he looked to an earlier letter from Theo, telling him that his authority within the gallery was increasing, and that he would soon be able to set prices himself.[77] Gauguin was terribly disappointed when he learned the circumstances in which the telegram was composed. Andries rushed to let Doctor Gachet know that Theo was very ill: "Since yesterday my brother-in-law van Gogh has been in such a state of over-excitement that we are seriously worried. ... The over-excitement is caused by a difference of opinion with his employers, as a result of which he wants to establish himself on his own without further waiting. The memory of his brother haunts him to such a degree that he resents everybody who does not agree with his ideas. My sister is exhausted and does not know what to do."[78] On October 12, Theo was hospitalized at the Dubois nursing home. Two days later, he was transferred to Doctor Blanche's clinic in Passy, where Gérard de Nerval was treated in his time. He was treated by both Antoine Emile Blanche, a highly regarded psychiatrist, and Doctor Meuriot. The doctors prescribed total rest; it was ironic that Theo received the same treatment as Vincent during the various attacks of his illness. In the nursing home, his condition stabilized and even improved.

Wil, who was informed of the situation by Jo, came to support her sister-in-law during Theo's hospitalization. Jo worried about her husband's condition—with good reason. Andries relates the terrible truth to his parents: "Rivet [Theo and Vincent's doctor in Paris] said that his case is far worse than Vincent's, and that there is not a spark of hope."[79]

News of Theo's illness spread throughout the artists' community of Paris, affecting all those who valued his kindness and recognized his devotion to his brother and other artists. Albert Aurier writes: "All we can do now is to perform our duty as friends—perhaps also hope."[80] As for his employers, at first it appeared they would help their manager during his illness. They told Tersteeg—who had come to Paris on October 21 and had gone to the sick man's bedside with Doctor Gachet—that they had not accepted Theo's resignation, given in a moment of insanity. They promised to keep him on until the end of the year.[81] However, Maurice Joyant, Theo's successor at the gallery, revealed in his book on Toulouse-Lautrec, what Boussod and Valadon had said to him about the employee who had dedicated his life to them: "Our manager, van Gogh, a madman of sorts, like his brother the painter, is in a mental asylum. You go and replace him, do as you please. He has accumulated appalling things by modern painters which are the shame of the firm. As a matter of fact there are also a few Corots, Rousseaus, Daubignys, but we have taken away that stock from there. . . . You will also find a certain number of canvases by landscape painter, Claude Monet, who is beginning to sell a little in America, but he makes too many. . . . All the rest are horrors; try to manage and don't ask us for anything, otherwise we'll close the shop."[82] Theo's relentless battle to have modern art accepted in that inflexible house had all been for nothing.

Utrecht: Theo's Final Days

WITH THEO'S HEALTH STABILIZED, his wife took him to Holland so that he could be cared for closer to his family. Jo's father petitioned the Dutch court, which officially granted Theo the right to be committed to an appropriate medical institution for a year. Accompanied by his wife and two employees from Doctor Blanche's clinic, Theo traveled by night. On November 18, he was admitted to the Willem Arntz Huis psychiatric clinic, in Utrecht, and it was there that he would spend the few months he had left to live.

Theo's behavior became very alarming once again: he would get confused and express incomprehensible thoughts in several languages; he was also inclined to try to rend his clothing. As in Paris, he had a persistent cough. He also had difficulty moving: his right foot was swollen after a fall. At times he was incontinent.

His condition remained virtually unchanged over the following days. He always looked pitiable and continued to refuse to eat. The doctors applied a treatment of baths and administered tranquilizers for anxiety, as well as other drugs. On November 24, he seemed calmer, so the specialists allowed a few visitors. One was Doctor Van der Maaten, who had auscultated him in Paris; he found that Theo's condition had deteriorated.

Jo was shattered by the illness that was ravaging her husband. Adding to the pain, Theo no longer recognized his wife. And his words were unintelligible.

During one of his frequent fits, Theo smashed chairs and a table, and damaged a mattress and various other objects. He was too overwrought for the doctors to allow him any more visits, so Jo sent a bouquet of flowers, which he immediately destroyed. Day by day, he was wasting away, eating nothing, and when he did eat, he sometimes vomited. In early January 1891, a doctor, hoping to get his patient's attention, read him an article on Vincent that had appeared in the *Handelsblad*; Theo reacted only to his brother's name.

And though he responded to Vincent's name, there was no improvement in his condition. Jo and Theo's sister visited him on January 13, with no effect. By the end of the cold, winter month, Theo succumbed to his illness; he was thirty-three years old. He died just six months after Vincent's suicide.

MANY OF VINCENT'S BIOGRAPHERS, relying on contemporary reports, maintain that Theo died of grief, because he was unable to recover from the loss of his brother. In 1940, Doctor Victor Doiteau studied Theo's illness and inferred Bright's disease, a disease of the kidneys.[83] Today, that diagnosis no longer fits with Theo's medical file, which reveals that he had been suffering for years from a general paralysis,[84] the last stage of syphilis.

The report of his first examination, carried out upon his arrival in Utrecht, describes: "A state of megalomanic delirium, accompanied by 'delusions of grandeur' and creeping paralysis, or *dementia paralytica*."[85] This diagnosis echoes that of Doctor Meuriot of Doctor Blanche's clinic, which was sent to the Dutch clinic: "In Paris, the patient was admitted suffering from creeping paralysis."[86] The last examination of Theo in Utrecht confirmed the two previous ones; it was definitely a galloping *dementia paralytica*, the symptoms of which are: disturbances in walking and speaking, changeable psychic blitheness, excitement and destructive urges, incontinence, and disorientation.

On January 28, 1891, Theo was buried, in a very intimate ceremony, in the cemetery of Utrecht, a city with which he had no connection. Hearing of his death, many artists praised his goodness, honesty, courage, and erudition: "We have learned of the death of Theo van Gogh, that sympathetic and intelligent expert who exerted himself so greatly so that the public would know of the works of today's most audacious independent artists."[87] Theo's faithful friend Camille Pissarro confides to his son: "Poor boy, he is no longer suffering; it was pitiful to know that he was mad, he who was once so intelligent and so active!"[88] Even Paul Gauguin, who was rather sparing of compliments, writes his friend Daniel de Monfreid: "When Goupil's [Theo] van Gogh went mad, I was screwed. . . . Only van Gogh knew how to sell and how to foster a clientele; not a single person today can tempt the clientele."[89]

EPILOGUE

"I FEAR NO ONE WILL BE ABLE TO CURE HIM completely. That mind has for so long been preoccupied with things our society today has made
impossible to solve & which he, with his kind heart &
tremendous energy, nevertheless fought against. His efforts
have not been in vain, but he may never be able to witness
their fruits, for it will be too late by the time people understand what he was expressing in his paintings. He is one of the
most progressive of the painters & even I, who am so close to
him, find him difficult to understand. He holds such sweeping
ideas on questions of what is humane and how we should
regard the world, that one first has to relinquish all one's conventional ideas in order to grasp what he means. But one day

MEIJER DE HAAN, *Theo van Gogh*, 1889.
Van Gogh Museum, Amsterdam

he will be understood."[1] Theo's assesment of his brother was prescient indeed. Despite the torments and the conflicts, Vincent's oeuvre, which is so admired in our time, proved to be one of the important foundations of modern art. It was a body of work that was still private when Theo died, since he had not achieved the goal he had set for himself—to make sure Vincent's exceptional genius was recognized.

Johanna continued her husband's fight, and she succeeded. First, she saw to it that the van Gogh family accepted her son as Vincent's sole heir. She soon left her apartment in Paris, unable to bear the places that so painfully reminded her of her husband. She moved to the Dutch city of Bussum, where she opened a small family boardinghouse, which she decorated with the dozens of Vincent's canvases she had gathered together. She then turned to organizing exhibitions, with the help of some of the brothers' friends. In 1892, Emile Bernard, with Johanna's support, showed sixteen paintings. It was not until 1901, when the gallery Bernheim-Jeune displayed works by van Gogh, that he would begin to be recognized by painters such as Henri Matisse and Maurice de Vlaminck and to arouse the interest of the Parisian public. That same year, Johanna married the painter and art critic Johan Cohen-Gosschalk. Together, in 1905, they organized one of the first important exhibitions of the work of Vincent van Gogh at Amsterdam's Stedelijk Museum. Indicating Vincent's increasing importance and popularity, forged van Goghs were already circulating; Theo had been the only person in the world who knew every one of Vincent's paintings. Widowed again in 1912, Johanna continued her struggle alone. To meet her living expenses, she sold a few paintings to a Dutch collector, Hélène Kröller-Muller, who would own a great many of Vincent's drawings. The value of the painter's works began to appreciate. From 1915 to 1920, Johanna lived in the United States. When she died, in 1925 at the age of sixty-three, the torch passed to her son.

Vincent Willem van Gogh, an engineer, now was in control of the treasure left him by his godfather and father. On the occasion of the hundredth anniversary of Vincent's birth, Theo's son exhibited his father's private collection, which numbered, in addition to Vincent's canvases, slightly more than one hundred paintings. These included a Corot, Daubignys, Gauguins, Manets, a Millet, Monticellis, Pissarros—father and son—Raffaëllis, Toulouse-Lautrecs, and more. Because of his limited budget, Theo had purchased few works, but over the years he and Vincent had traded with many artists, including Bernard and Guillaumin. They had received paintings as gifts: Gauguin gave Theo a canvas of Vincent painting sunflowers; Meijer de Haan did his portrait and gave it to him in thanks for putting him up at Rue Lepic. A few works bear dedications to Theo, but all bear witness to both his boldness and his judiciousness as a collector.

In the face of the ever-increasing popularity of Vincent's paintings with professionals and amateurs alike, his godson decided to sell his works to the Dutch government for a huge sum in 1962. The *peintre maudit* now has his own museum, and his fame worldwide is such that today his paintings go for staggering prices. Johanna, like Theo, was right to believe in her brother-in-law's work. Driven by her love for her husband, she did everything in her power to promote Vincent's oeuvre. Fortunately, she did not listen to those—including her brother Andries—who believed his paintings would never be worth anything. Through the recognition Vincent would receive, she meant to honor Theo's memory and his generosity.

Far from this commercial frenzy, two men, two broth- ers, lie in the little cemetery at Auvers, joined in death as they had been in life. For eternity. In 1914, twenty-three years after her husband's death, Johanna had his remains taken to Auvers. Why did she wait so long? According to Johanna's statements, she received a revelation as she was reading a verse from the Bible: "What therefore God hath joined together, let not man put asunder," a conjecture that contin- ues to feed the myth of Theo and Vincent. Curiously, rather than repatriating Vincent to his native land, she elected to reunite the two men in Auvers.

It was to Johanna that we owe the first edition of Vincent's correspondence—more than six hundred letters that Theo had treasured over eighteen years. After Theo's death, Johanna threw herself into reading these letters, trying to bring back the beloved person she had lost too soon. She wanted to know about his life before they had met, penetrate his most intimate thoughts. "On the first evening I spent in our apartment, after my return, I began rereading these let- ters, for I knew they would allow me to be in his company again, and night after night, I found in them a consolation for my immense grief. In those days, it was not Vincent but only Theo whom I sought."[2] The volume she created was an expur- gated version, which has since been completed, and today art historians and others question the chronological order, or dates, of some of the letters. Vincent's correspondence has still not been entirely elucidated.

What did she find in that correspondence that made her decide to bring her husband's remains back to France, when she was living in Holland? Perhaps it was a trace of what existed between the two brothers, that very intimate bond that was necessary to their survival.

Tragedy beset the van Gogh family again and again. Anna, who had endured the loss of two of her sons within the same year, was subject to more loss throughout her life. Her third son, Cor, would kill himself in South Africa. As for Wil, Theo and Vincent's favorite sister, she went insane and ended her days in an asylum.

IN THE LITTLE CEMETERY AT AUVERS, not far from the wheat fields, you can find two identical gravestones. They are very simple, undecorated, covered only by draping ivy. Ivy—the plant that signifies: "I cling or I die."

FIG. 1: *Gravestones of Vincent van Gogh and Theo van Gogh in Auvers-sur-Oise*

NOTES

Translation of letters by Robert Harrison are marked *RH*. All other transla-
tions are by Alexandra Bonfante-Warren.

Chapter 1

1. The name "van Gogh" is believed to be derived from the family's ancestral
   city, Goch, today in Germany, not far from the Dutch border. Those
   descendants who emigrated to the Netherlands seem to have moved in the
   circles of the local nobility.
2. Unpublished letter of Dorus to Theo, April 29, 1883, b2243V/1982.
   Fondation Vincent van Gogh.
3. "Dominie" is the form of address for pastors in Brabant.
4. B. J. Stokvis, *Nasporingen omtrent Vincent van Gogh in Brabant* (Amsterdam:
   S. L. Van Looy, 1926).
5. Ibid.
6. Ibid.
7. Elisabeth du Quesne-van Gogh, *Vincent van Gogh raconté par sa soeur*
   (Paris: Hazan, 1982).
8. Marc Edo Tralbaut, *Van Gogh, le mal aimé* (Lausanne: Edita, 1969).
9. Letter from Vincent to Theo in Vincent van Gogh, *The Complete Letters of
   Vincent van Gogh* (Boston: Little, Brown & Co., 1991), 573 F.

10. Ibid., 11 N.

11. His younger brother, Cornelius Vincent, known as Cor, was born in 1867.

Chapter 2

1. Anna gives Theo news of her in an unpublished letter of January 9, 1873, b2593V/1982.

2. B. J. Stokvis, *Nasporingen omtrent Vincent van Gogh in Brabant* (Amsterdam: S. L. Van Looy, 1926).

3. Letter from Vincent to Theo in Vincent van Gogh, *The Complete Letters of Vincent van Gogh* (Boston: Little, Brown & Co., 1991), 10 N.

4. Letter from Vincent to Theo, *The Complete Letters*, 1 N.

5. Dorus reveals this in an unpublished letter to Theo, February 19, 1873, b2604V/1982. Fondation Vincent van Gogh.

6. Letter from Vincent to Theo, *The Complete Letters*, 3 N.

7. Quoted from an article in *Journal des Beaux-Arts et de la littérature* (Brussels; January 31, 1869).

8. Ibid.

9. Letter from Vincent to Theo, *The Complete Letters*, 3 N.

10. Unpublished letter from Anna to Theo, January 9, 1873, b2593V/1982. Fondation Vincent van Gogh.

11. Ibid., in a long postscript from Dorus.

12. Ibid.

13. Unpublished letter from Dorus to Theo, January 24, 1873, b2596V/1982. Fondation Vincent van Gogh.

14. Unpublished letter from Dorus to Theo, February 19, 1873.

15. Johanna van Gogh-Bonger and V. W. van Gogh, eds., *Verzamelde Brieven van Vincent van Gogh* (Amsterdam: Wereld Bibliothek, 1952–54), T43.

16. *Journal 1996*, Amsterdam, Van Gogh Museum, 1997.

17. Unpublished letter from Dorus to Theo, August 11, 1875, b2352V/1982. Fondation Vincent van Gogh.

18. Letter from Vincent to Theo, January 1874, *The Complete Letters*, 13 N.

19. Ibid.

20. Albert Plasschaert (1917), quoted in John Sillevis, Ronald de Leeuw, and Charles Dumas, *L'École de La Haye: Les maîtres hollandais du XIXe siècle* (Paris: Grand Palais, 1983), 131. E. J. Van Wisselingh was an excellent dealer in Amsterdam. Cor, or Cornelius, Marinus van Gogh, an uncle of Vincent and Theo, ran a gallery bearing his name in Amsterdam.

21. Unpublished letter from Dorus to Theo, December 11, 1873, b2674V/1982. Fondation Vincent van Gogh.

22. Letter from Vincent to Theo, *The Complete Letters*, 21 N.

23. Unpublished letter from Dorus to Theo, October 5, 1874, b2724V/1982. Fondation Vincent van Gogh.

24. Unpublished letter from Anna to Theo, November 18, 1874, b2734V/1982. Fondation Vincent van Gogh.

25. Unpublished letter from Anna to Theo, October 28, 1874, b2729V/1982. Fondation Vincent van Gogh.

26. Unpublished letter from Dorus to Theo, October 28, 1874, b2728V/1982. Fondation Vincent van Gogh.

27. Unpublished letter from Dorus to Theo, July 8, 1875, b2346V/1982. Fondation Vincent van Gogh. Transl. by RH.

28. Unpublished letter from Dorus to Theo, July 8, 1875, b2346V/1982. Fondation Vincent van Gogh.

29. Letter from Vincent to Theo, June 19, 1875, *The Complete Letters*, 28 N.

30. Ibid.

31. Letter from Theo to Vincent, *The Complete Letters*, 36a N. Vincent returned this letter to Theo with his annotations and reply on the back. Theo kept it, as he did all his brother's letters.

32. Letter from Vincent to Theo, *The Complete Letters*, 36a N.

33. Letter from Vincent to Theo, *The Complete Letters*, 40 N.

34. Letter from Vincent to Theo, *The Complete Letters*, 41 N.

35. Unpublished letter from Laurent Vink to Theo, July 21, 1875. Fondation Vincent van Gogh.

36. Letter from Vincent to Theo, *The Complete Letters*, 38 N.

37. Unpublished letter from Dorus to Theo, March 31, 1876, b0955V/1962. Fondation Vincent van Gogh. Transl. by RH.

38. Unpublished letter from Dorus to Theo, November 18, 1876, b2794V/1982. Fondation Vincent van Gogh. Transl by ABW.

39. Letter from Vincent to Theo, *The Complete Letters*, 98 N.

Chapter 3

1. Philippe Bouin and Christian-Philippe Chanut, *Histoire française des foires et des expositions universelles* (Paris: Editions de Nesle, 1980), 100–101.

2. Ibid., 99.

3. Rodolphe Walter, "L'Exposition universelle de 1878, ou Amours et Haines d'Emile Zola," *L'Œil* no. 280 (November 1978): 38–45.

4. Emile Zola, Letter from Paris, 38, "L'école française de la peinture à l'Exposition de 1878," *Le Messager de l'Europe* (July 1878).

5. Unpublished letter from Anna to Theo, May 8, 1878, b0976V/1962. Fondation Vincent van Gogh.

6. Letter from Vincent to Theo in Vincent van Gogh, *The Complete Letters of Vincent van Gogh* (Boston: Little, Brown & Co., 1991), 122 N.

7. Unpublished letter from Dorus to Theo, May 10, 1878, b0977V/1962. Fondation Vincent van Gogh. Transl. by RH

8. In the letter, Anna quotes Cent's advice to Theo. Unpublished letter from Anna to Theo, June 7, 1878, b0980V/1962. Fondation Vincent van Gogh. Transl. by RH.

9. Unpublished letter from Cent van Gogh to Theo, October 7, 1878, b5342V/1994. Fondation Vincent van Gogh.

10. Letter from Vincent to Theo, *The Complete Letters*, 126 N.

11. Letter from Vincent to Theo, *The Complete Letters*, 129 N.

12. Unpublished letter from Dorus to Theo, April 23, 1879, b2469V/1982. Fondation Vincent van Gogh. Transl by ABW.

13. Unpublished letter from Dorus to Theo, August 7, 1879, b2488V/1982. Fondation Vincent van Gogh.

14. Unpublished letter from Dorus and Anna to Theo, August 10, 1879, b2491V/1982. Fondation Vincent van Gogh.

15. Unpublished letter from Dorus to Theo, May 28, 1879, b2480V/1982. Fondation Vincent van Gogh.

16. Unpublished letter from Dorus to Theo, May 30, 1879, b2481V/1982. Fondation Vincent van Gogh.

17. Unpublished letter from Anna to Theo, Paris, June 2, 1879, b2483V/1982. Fondation Vincent van Gogh.

18. Letter from Theo to Vincent, 132 N.

19. Letter from Vincent to Theo, August 1879, 132. Transl. by RH.

20. Letter from Vincent to Theo, *The Complete Letters*, 133 F.

21. Unpublished letter from Anna to Theo, July 5, 1880, b2494V/1982. Fondation Vincent van Gogh.

22. Unpublished letter from Dorus to Theo, August 5, 1881, b2236V/1962. Fondation Vincent van Gogh.

23. To give the reader an idea, a beginning teacher earned seventy-five francs a month.

24. Unpublished document, b4601V/1982. Fondation Vincent van Gogh.

25. Sophie Monneret, *L'Impressionisme et son époque* (Paris: Robert Laffont, Collection Bouquins, 1987), 293.

26. Letter from Andries Bonger to his parents, August 27, 1881, quoted in Leo Jansen and Jan Robert, eds., *Brief Happiness: The Correspondence of Theo van Gogh and Jo Bonger* (Amsterdam: Van Gogh Museum and Waanders Publishers, 1999), 11.

27. Letter from Theo to Jo Bonger, *Brief Happiness*, 141.

28. Unpublished letter from Theo to Lies, October 13, 1885, b0903V/1962. Fondation Vincent van Gogh. Transl. by RH.

29. Unpublished letter from Theo to Lies, December 28, 1885, b0904V/1962. Fondation Vincent van Gogh.

30. Maurice Donnay, *Autour du Chat noir* (Paris: Grasset, 1926), 56.
31. Letter from Vincent to Theo, *The Complete Letters*, 259 N.
32. Letter from Vincent to Theo, *The Complete Letters*, 262 N.
33. Letter from Vincent to Theo, *The Complete Letters*, 267 N.
34. Letter from Vincent to Theo, *The Complete Letters*, 263 N.
35. Letter from Vincent to Theo, *The Complete Letters*, 260 N.
36. Letter from Vincent to Theo, 260 N.
37. Letter from Vincent to Theo, *The Complete Letters*, 288 N.
38. Letter from Theo to Vincent, *The Complete Letters*, 169 N.
39. Letter from Vincent to Theo, *The Complete Letters*, 332 N.
40. Unpublished letter from Dorus and Anna to Theo, October 1, 1883, b2245V/1982. Fondation Vincent van Gogh.
41. Letter from Vincent to Theo, *The Complete Letters*, 333 N.
42. Ibid.
43. Letter from Vincent to Theo, *The Complete Letters*, 332 N.
44. Letter from Vincent to Theo, *The Complete Letters*, 333 N.

Chapter 4

1. Unpublished letter from Dorus to Theo, August 22, 1884, b2256V/1982. Fondation Vincent van Gogh.
2. Letter from Vincent to Theo in Vincent van Gogh, *The Complete Letters of Vincent van Gogh* (Boston: Little, Brown & Co., 1991), 358 N.
3. Letter from Vincent to Theo, 358 N.
4. Letter from Vincent to Theo, *The Complete Letters*, 358 N.
5. John Rewald, "Theo van Gogh, Goupil and the Impressionists," *Gazette des Beaux-Arts* (January 1973): 5.
6. Ibid.
7. Unpublished letter from Dorus to Theo, December 30, 1884, b2264V/1982. Fondation Vincent van Gogh.
8. Pierre Leprohon, *Vincent van Gogh* (Le Cannet: Editions Corymbe, 1972), 163.
9. Letter from Vincent to Theo, *The Complete Letters*, 362 N.
10. Letter from Vincent to Theo, *The Complete Letters*, 364 N.
11. Viviane Forrester, *Van Gogh ou l'enterrement dans les blés* (Paris: Editions du Seuil, 1983), 193.
12. Unpublished letter from Dorus to Theo, March 25, 1885, b2269V/1982. Fondation Vincent van Gogh.
13. Henk Bonger, "Un Amstellodamois à Paris," in *Liber Amicorum Karel G. Boon* (Amsterdam: Sweets & Zeitlinger BV, 1974), 67.
14. Letter from Vincent to Theo, *The Complete Letters*, 398 N.

15. Unpublished letter from Theo to Cor, March 11, 1887, b0907V/1982. Fondation Vincent van Gogh.

16. Unpublished letter from Theo to Anna, April 22, 1885, b0900V/1962. Fondation Vincent van Gogh.

17. Unpublished letter from Theo to Anna, May 19, 1885, b0901V/1962. Fondation Vincent van Gogh.

18. Unpublished letter from Theo to Lies, October 13, 1885, b0903V/1962. Fondation Vincent van Gogh. Transl. by RH.

19. Letter from Vincent to Theo in V. W. van Gogh, *Letters of Vincent van Gogh, 1886–1890*, (London: The Scolar Press, Ltd., 1977), 439 F.

20. Letter from Andries Bonger to his parents, quoted in Leo Jansen and Jan Robert, eds., *Brief Happiness: The Correspondence of Theo van Gogh and Jo Bonger* (Van Gogh Museum and Waanders Publishers, 1999), 16.

21. Letter from Andries Bonger to his parents, quoted in *Brief Happiness*, 15.

22. Letter from Andries Bonger to his parents, *The Complete Letters*, 462 a.

23. Unpublished letter from Theo to Anna, June 1886 and July 1886, b0942V/1962. Fondation Vincent van Gogh. Transl. by RH.

24. Letter from Vincent to Theo, *The Complete Letters*, 460 N.

25. Letter from Andries Bonger to his parents, Paris, 1886, quoted in M. E. Tralbaut, "Andries Bonger, l'ami des frères Van Gogh," (Antwerp) *Van Goghiana* 1, (January 1963): 6.

26. Unpublished letter from Theo to Lies, May 15, 1887, b0912V/1962. Fondation Vincent van Gogh.

27. The van Gogh brothers spelled his name "Tangui."

28. Suzanne Valadon quoted in John Rewald, *Post-Impressionism: From Van Gogh to Gauguin* (New York: The Museum of Modern Art, 1956), 30.

29. Unpublished letter from Theo to Anna, February 28, 1887, b0906V/1962. Fondation Vincent van Gogh. Transl. by RH.

30. Unpublished letter from Theo to Wil, March 14, 1887, b0908V/1962. Fondation Vincent van Gogh. Transl. by RH.

31. Unpublished letter from Theo to Wil, April 25, 1887, b0911V/1962. Fondation Vincent van Gogh. Transl. by RH.

32. Unpublished letter from Theo to Lies, May 15, 1887, b0912V/1962. Fondation Vincent van Gogh. Transl. by RH.

33. Unpublished letter from Theo to Wil, February 24 and 26, 1888, b0914V/1962. Fondation Vincent van Gogh. Transl. by RH.

34. Unpublished letter from Theo to Wil, December 6, 1888, b0916V/1962. Fondation Vincent van Gogh.

35. Letter from Vincent to Wil, *The Complete Letters*, W4N.

36. Letter from Theo to Vincent, October 27, 1888, in Johanna van Gogh-Bonger and V. W. van Gogh, eds., *Verzamelde Brieven van Vincent van Gogh* (Amsterdam: Wereld Bibliothek, 1952–54), vol. 4,. T3.

37. Rewald, *Post-Impressionism*, 7. This canvas has not been identified.
38. Gustave Kahn, *Au temps du pointillisme* (Paris) *Mercure de France* (May 1, 1924): 18.
39. Claude Monet quoted in John Rewald, "Theo van Gogh, Goupil and the Impressionists," 23.
40. Rewald, "Theo van Gogh, Goupil and the Impressionists," 10.
41. Unpublished letter from Theo to Camille Pissarro, Paris, January 30, 1888. Archives of the département of Val-d'Oise.
42. Letter from Camille Pissarro to Lucien Pissarro, Eragny, August 28, 1887 in Camille Pissarro, *Lettres à son fils Lucien* (Paris: Albin Michel, 1950), 161.
43. Rewald, "Theo van Gogh, Goupil and the Impressionists," 15.
44. Letter from Camille Pissarro to Theo, September 17, 1888, b0814V/1962. Fondation Vincent van Gogh.
45. Letter from Monet to Durand-Ruel, September 24, 1888, cited in Rewald, "Theo van Gogh, Goupil and the Impressionists," 23.
46. Letter from Camille Pissarro to Lucien Pissarro, Paris, July 12, 1888, in Camille Pissarro, *Lettres à son fils Lucien*, 156.
47. Hermann Schlittgen, *Erinnerungen* (Munich: A. Langen 1926), 199–200.
48. The exact canvas sold is not known.
49. Letter from Vincent to Theo, *The Complete Letters*, 550 F.
50. Unpublished letter from Theo to Wil, December 6, 1888, b0916V/1962. Fondation Vincent van Gogh.
51. Rewald, "Theo van Gogh, Goupil and the Impressionists," 15.

Chapter 5

1. Unpublished letter from Theo to Anna, December 21, 1888, b0917V/1962. Fondation Vincent van Gogh. Transl. by RH.
2. Unpublished letter from Anna to Theo, December 22, 1888, b2389V/1982. Fondation Vincent van Gogh. Transl. by RH.
3. Jean-Claude Bologne, *Histoire du sentiment amoureux* (Paris: Flammarion, 1998).
4. Unpublished letter from Anna to Theo, December 22, 1888, b2389V/1982. Fondation Vincent van Gogh.
5. Unpublished letter from Theo Lies, April 19, 1887, b910V/1962. Fondation Vincent van Gogh. Transl. by RH.
6. She was the aunt of the future architect of the Stedelijk Museum in Amsterdam.
7. This description of Johanna van Gogh-Bonger is by her son in *Verzamelde Brieven van Vincent van Gogh* (Amsterdam: Wereld Bibliothek 1952–54), lix.

8. Letter from Jo to Theo in Leo Jansen and Jan Robert, eds., *Brief Happiness: The Correspondence of Theo van Gogh and Jo Bonger* (Amsterdam: Van Gogh Museum and Waanders Publishers, 1999), 234.

9. Unpublished letter from Anna to Theo, December 22, 1888, b2389V/1982. Fondation Vincent van Gogh.

10. Unpublished letter from Theo to Lies, April 19, 1887, b0910V/1962. Fondation Vincent van Gogh.

11. Unpublished letter from Theo to Lies, December 24, 1888, b0918V/1962. Fondation Vincent van Gogh.

12. Unpublished letter from Theo to Anna, b0917V/1962. Fondation Vincent van Gogh.

13. Jo van Gogh-Bonger quoted in *Verzamelde Brieven van Vincent van Gogh*, xlv.

14. Letter from Gauguin to Theo quoted in John Rewald, *Post-Impressionism: From Van Gogh to Gauguin*, (New York: The Museum of Modern Art, 1956), 236.

15. Letter from Emile Bernard to Albert Aurier, written four days after the event, quoted in Rewald, *Post-Impressionism*, 265–6.

16. Ibid.

17. Letter from Theo to Jo, *Brief Happiness*, 67.

18. Letter from Theo to Jo, *Brief Happiness*, 70.

19. Letter from Theo to Jo, *Brief Happiness*, 74.

20. Letter from Theo to Jo, *Brief Happiness*, 76.

21. Vincent van Gogh quoted in Viviane Forrester, *Van Gogh, ou, l'enterrement dans les blés* (Paris: Le Seuil, 1983).

22. Charles Mauron, *Van Gogh, études psychocritiques* (Paris: José Corti, 1976).

23. Letter from Theo to Jo, *Brief Happiness*, 76.

24. Ibid.

25. Letter from Bernard to Aurier, quoted in part in Rewald, *Post-Impressionism*, 267–8.

26. Letter from Theo to Jo, *Brief Happiness*, 81.

27. Ibid.

28. Ibid.

29. Letter from Theo to Jo, *Brief Happines*, 22.

30. Letter from Theo to Jo, *Brief Happiness*, 88.

31. Letter from Vincent to Theo in Vincent Van Gogh, *The Complete Letters of Vincent van Gogh* (Boston: Little, Brown & Co., 1991), 567 F.

32. Unpublished letter from Wil to Jo, March 8, 1889, b2397V/1982. Fondation Vincent van Gogh.

33. Unpublished letter from Anna to Theo, March 12, 1889, b2934V/1982. Fondation Vincent van Gogh.

34. Letter from Theo to Vincent, *The Complete Letters*, T 4.

35. Letter from Theo to Jo, *Brief Happiness*, 222.

36. Unpublished letter from Wil to Theo, March 16, 1889, b2392V/1982. Fondation Vincent van Gogh.

37. Letter from Theo to Jo, *Brief Happiness*, 223.

38. Unpublished letter from Theo to Jo, March 14, 1889, b2047V/1982. Fondation Vincent van Gogh.

39. Letter from Pastor Salles to Theo, April 19, 1889, b1050V/1962. Fondation Vincent van Gogh.

40. Letter from Theo to Vincent, *The Complete Letters*, T 5.

41. Letter from Theo to Jo, *Brief Happiness*, 160.

42. Ibid.

43. Letter from Theo to Vincent, *The Complete Letters*, T 5.

44. Ibid.

45. Pissarro quoted in John Rewald, *Camille Pissarro* (Paris: Cercle d'Art, 1989).

46. Letter from Jo to Anna, June 7, 1889, bV/1982. Fondation Vincent van Gogh.

47. Ibid.

48. Letter from Jo to Vincent, *The Complete Letters*, T 8.

49. Letter from Jo to Theo, *Brief Happiness*, 90.

50. Unpublished letter from Jo to Wil, August 23, 1889, b0944V/1982. Fondation Vincent van Gogh.

51. Letter from Theo to Vincent, *The Complete Letters*, T 9. Chromos are lithographs.

52. Letter from Theo to Vincent, *The Complete Letters*, T 10.

53. Letter from Jo to Vincent, *The Complete Letters*, T 11.

54. Letter from Theo to Vincent, *The Complete Letters*, T 12.

55. Y. Knibiehlerp, "Corps et coeurs," in Geneviève Fraisse and Michèle Perrot, eds., *Histoire des femmes, Le XIXe siècle* (Paris: Plon, 1991).

56. Letter from Vincent to Jo and Theo, n.d., Vincent van Gogh, *Correspondance générale* (Paris: Gallimard, Collection Biblos, 1990), 599F.

57. Ibid.

58. Letter from Theo to Vincent, *The Complete Letters*, T 14.

59. Letter from Theo to Vincent, T 12, quoted in Theo van Gogh, *Lettres à son frere Vincent* (Amsterdam: N. v. Maatschappij).

60. David Sweetman, *Une vie de Vincent van Gogh* (Paris: Presses de la Renaissance, 1990).

61. Letter from Theo to Vincent, Sept. 5, 1889, T 16.

62. Letter from Theo to Vincent, *The Complete Letters*, T 18.

63. Ibid.

64. Letter from Theo to Vincent, *The Complete Letters*, T 19.

65. Letter from Theo to Vincent, *The Complete Letters*, T 22.

66. Letter from Theo to Vincent, *The Complete Letters*, T 24.

67. Letter from Vincent to Octave Maus, November 20, 1889, quoted in Rewald, *Post-Impressionism*, 342.

68. Letter from Theo to Vincent, *The Complete Letters*, T 25.
69. Henry de Groux quoted in Rewald, *Post-Impressionism*, 374.
70. Albert Aurier, "Les isolés, Vincent van Gogh," (Paris) *Mercure de France* (January 1890).
71. Letter from Theo to Vincent, *The Complete Letters*, T 27.
72. Letter from Vincent to Theo, *The Complete Letters* 625.
73. Letter from Jo to Vincent, *The Complete Letters*, T 26.
74. Letter from Theo to Vincent, *The Complete Letters*, T 29.
75. Letter from Theo to Vincent, *The Complete Letters*, T 31.
76. Letter from Theo to Vincent, *The Complete Letters*, T 32.
77. Ibid.
78. Letter from Theo to Vincent, May 3, 1890, T 33.
79. Letter from Vincent to Theo, late February 1884, 358 N 80. Letter from Theo to Vincent, March 29, 1890, T 31.

Chapter 6

1. Theo van Gogh quoted in Paul Gachet, *Deux amis des impressionistes, le Dr. Gachet et Mürer* (Paris: Editions des Musées nationaux, 1956), 110.
2. Ibid., 111.
3. Letter from Theo to Vincent in Vincent van Gogh, *The Complete Letters of Vincent van Gogh* (Boston: Little, Brown & Co., 1991), T 35.
4. Unpublished letter from Theo to Wil, June 2, 1890, b0931V/1962. Fondation Vincent van Gogh.
5. Letter from Theo to Vincent, *The Complete Letters*, T 36.
6. Letter from Theo to Vincent, *The Complete Letters*, T 35.
7. Adeline Carrié, "Les souvenirs d'Adeline Ravoux sur le séjourde Vincent van Gogh à Auvers-sur-Oise". *Les Cahiers de Van Gogh*, no. 1 (1956): 7–17.
8. Annie Bonger quoted in Henk Bonger, "Un Amstellodamois à Paris," in *Liber Amicorum Karel G. Boon* (Amsterdam: Sweets & Zeitlinger BV, 1974), 69.
9. Unpublished letter from Theo to Anna and Wil, June 29, 1890, b0932V/1962. Fondation Vincent van Gogh.
10. Letter from Theo to Vincent, *The Complete Letters*, T 39.
11. G. Kraus, *Les liens entre Theo et Vincent van Gogh* (Amsterdam: Fondation Kröller-Muller et J. M. Meulenhoff, 1954), 31.
12. Letter from Theo to Vincent, *The Complete Letters*, T 39.
13. Ibid.
14. Letter from Vincent to Theo and Jo, *The Complete Letters*, 646 F.
15. Ibid.
16. G. Kraus, *Les Liens*, 32.

17. Letter from Theo to Vincent in V. W. van Gogh, *Letters of Vincent van Gogh, 1886–1890*, (London: The Scolar Press, Ltd., 1977), T 40.

18. Letter from Vincent to Theo and Jo, *Letters of Vincent van Gogh*, 648 F.

19. Letter from Theo to Vincent, *The Complete Letters*, T 41.

20. Letter from Theo to Vincent, July 22, 1890. *Der Spiegel* (January 22, 1990).

21. Letter from Paul Gauguin to Theo, July 7, 1890, GAC 25, in Douglas Cooper, *Paul Gauguin: quarante-cinq lettres à Vincent, Theo et Jo van Gogh* (Amsterdam: Collection Rijksmuseum Vincent van Gogh, 1983), 183. Theo sold Eugène Blot, a Paris art dealer, a canvas titled *Dog Running in the Grass* for two hundred francs, one hundred fifty francs of which went to the painter. The painting has not been identified.

22. Letter from Vincent to Jo and Theo, *The Complete Letters*, 649 F.

23. Letter from Theo to Vincent, *The Complete Letters*, T 41.

24. Ibid.

25. Letter from Theo to Jo, July 22, 1890. *Der Spiegel* (January 22, 1990).

26. Letter from Theo to Jo in Leo Jansen and Jan Robert, eds., *Brief Happiness: The Correspondence of Theo van Gogh and Jo Bonger* (Van Gogh Museum and Waanders Publishers, 1999), 245.

27. Letter from Jo to Theo, *Brief Happiness*, 252.

28. Unpublished letter from Theo to Jo, *Brief Happiness*, 258.

29. Ibid.

30. Unpublished letter from Theo to Jo, *Brief Happiness*, 253.

31. Ibid.

32. Letter from Theo to Anna and Wil, July 22, 1890, b0933V/1962. Fondation Vincent van Gogh.

33. Letter from Theo to Jo, *Brief Happiness*, 253.

34. Ibid.

35. Letter from Theo to Jo, *Brief Happiness*, 265.

36. Letter from Jo to Theo, *Brief Happiness*, 267.

37. Letter from Jo to Theo, *Brief Happiness*, 251.

38. Letter from Theo to Vincent, July 22, 1890, T41A. Transl. by RH.

39. Letter from Theo to Jo, Auvers, *Brief Happiness*, 269–70.

40. Letter from Theo to Jo, *Brief Happiness*, 279.

41. Letter from Vincent to Theo, *The Complete Letters*, 652 F. This is the letter he had on him on July 29.

42. Letter from Camille Pissarro to Theo, July 30, 1890, in Jeannine Bailly-Herzberg, *Correspondance de Camille Pissarro, 1886–1890* (Paris: Editions de Valhermeil), 54.

43. Emile Bernard, "L'enterrement de Vincent van Gogh," *Arts-Documents* (February 1953).

44. Letter from Theo to Jo, *Brief Happiness*, 279.

45. Ibid.

46. Letter from Theo to Vincent, July 22, 1890, T 41A. Transl. by RH. The letter, a reply to one of Vincent's, was originally sent to Amsterdam, from where Jo sent it back to her husband. Its whereabouts are today unknown.

47. Ibid.

48. Letter from Jo to Theo, *Brief Happiness*, 264.

49. Letter from Jo to Theo, *Brief Happiness*, 277.

50. Kraus, *Les liens*, 29.

51. Letter from Vincent to Theo, *The Complete Letters*, 651 F.

52. Letter from Theo to Anna, August 1, 1890, b0934V/1962. Fondation Vincent van Gogh. Transl. by RH.

53. Letter from Theo to Jo, *Brief Happiness*, 270.

54. Letter from Theo to Anna, August 1, 1890, b0934V/1962. Fondation Vincent van Gogh.

55. Letter from Theo to Doctor Gachet, Amsterdam, August 12, 1890, in Paul Gachet, *Lettres impressionists* (Paris: Grasset, 1957), 151, and *Deux amis des impressionistes*, 122–3.

56. Unpublished letter from Joan and Anna van Houten and Wil and Lies van Gogh to Theo, August 1890, b2217V/1982. Fondation Vincent van Gogh.

57. Unpublished letter from Theo to Anna and Wil, August 11, 1890, b0935V/1962. Fondation Vincent van Gogh.

58. Letter from Theo to Doctor Gachet, September 12, 1890 in Gachet, *Lettres impressionistes*, 151.

59. Unpublished letter from Theo to Anna, August 24, 1890, b0936V/1962. Fondation Vincent van Gogh. Transl. by RH.

60. Theo's last letter to Doctor Gachet, September 12, 1890 in Gachet, *Deux amis des Impressionistes*, 153–5.

61. Letter from Theo to Albert Aurier, August 27, 1890 in John Rewald, *Post-Impressionism: From Van Gogh to Gauguin*, (New York: The Museum of Modern Art, 1956), 412.

62. Letter from Theo to Doctor Gachet, September 12, 1890 in Paul Gachet, *Deux amis des impressionistes*, 153–5.

63. Unpublished letter from Theo to Anna and Wil, August 24, 1890, b0936V/1962. Fondation Vincent van Gogh. Transl. by RH.

64. Ibid.

65. Rewald, *Post-Impressionism*, 414.

66. Unpublished letter from Theo to Camille Pissarro, September 30, 1890. Departmental Archives of the Val-d'Oise.

67. Letter from Theo to Emile Bernard quoted in Rewald, *Post-Impressionism*, 413.

68. Letter from Theo to Wil, September 27, 1890, b0947V/1962. Fondation Vincent van Gogh.

69. Letter from Theo to Wil in Jan Hulsker, *Vincent and Theo van Gogh: A Dual Biography* (Ann Arbor, Mich,: Fuller Publications, 1990), 452.

70. Unpublished letters from Theo to Camille Pissarro, September 30 and October 10, 1890. Departmental Archives of the Val-d'Oise.

71. Unpublished letter from Theo to Anna, Hulsker, *Dual Biography*, 452.

72. Bonger, "Un Amstellodamois à Paris," 69.

73. Letter from Theo to Doctor Gachet, September 12, 1890, in Paul Gachet, *Deux amis des impressionistes*, 153–5.

74. Unpublished letter from Theo to Wil, *Dual Biography*, 452.

75. Letter from Camille Pissarro to Lucien Pissarro, *Dual Biography*, 452.

76. Letter from Theo to Paul Gauguin in Rewald, *Post-Impressionism*, 414.

77. Letter from Paul Gauguin to Theo, Le Pouldu, July 7, 1890 in Cooper, *Paul Gauguin, quarante-cinq lettres à Vincent, Theo et Jo van Gogh*, 183.

78. Letter from Andries Bonger to Doctor Gachet, October 10, 1890, in Paul Gachet, *Deux amis des impressionists*, 125–6.

79. Letter from Andries Bonger to his parents, Hulsker, *A Dual Biography*, 453.

80. Letter from Albert Aurier to Doctor Gachet, October 22, 1890, in Paul Gachet, *Les 70 jours de van Gogh à Auvers* (Saint-Ouen-L'Aumône: Editions du Valhermeil, 1994), 292.

81. Hulsker, *A Dual Biography*, 454.

82. Maurice Joyant quoted in Hulsker, *Dual Biography*, 451–2.

83. Victor Doiteau, "À quel mal succomba Theodore van Gogh?" *Aesculape* vol. no. 30/1 (May 1940): 76–87.

84. P. H. A. Voskuil, "Hef medische dossier van Theo van Gogh" *Ned Tijdschr Geneeskd*, vol. 36, no. 36 (1992): 1777–79.

85. Theo van Gogh's medical file. Archives of the Willem Arntz Huis, Utrecht, and Fondation Vincent van Gogh.

86. Ibid.

87. Albert Aurier, *Mercure de France* (March 1891).

88. Letter from Camille Pissarro to Lucien Pissarro, February 1, 1891 in Camille Pissarro, *Lettres à son fils Lucien* (Paris: Albin Michel, 1950), 208.

89. Letter from Gauguin to Daniel de Monfreid, Tahiti, in Annie Joly-Segalen, *Lettres de Gauguin à Daniel de Monfreid* (Paris: Edition Etablie, 1950,) 58, 99.

Epilogue

1. Letter from Theo to Jo in Leo Jansen and Jan Robert, eds., *Brief Happiness: The Correspondence of Theo van Gogh and Jo Bonger* (Van Gogh Museum and Waanders Publishers, 1999), 146.

2. Jo quoted in David Sweetman, *Une vie de Vincent van Gogh* (Paris: Presses de la Renaissance, 1990).

SELECTED
BIBLIOGRAPHY

UNPUBLISHED SOURCES

Archives of the Fondation Vincent van Gogh, Amsterdam

Departmental Archives of Val-d'Oise, Pontoise, France

PUBLISHED SOURCES

Bonger, Henk. "Un Amstellodamois à Paris" in *Liber Amicorum Karel G. Boon*. Amsterdam: Sweets & Zeitlinger BV, 1974.

Bonger-van Gogh, Johanna, and V. W. van Gogh, eds. *Verzamelde Brieven van Vincent van Gogh*. 4 vols. Amsterdam: Wereld Bibliothek, 1952–54.

Cooper, Douglas. *Paul Gauguin: quarante-cinq lettres à Vincent, Theo et Jo van Gogh*. Amsterdam: Collection Rijksmuseum Vincent van Gogh, 1983.

Gachet, Paul. *Lettres impressionnistes*. Paris: Grasset, 1957.

Gauguin, Paul. *Lettres à sa femme et à ses amis*. Paris: Grasset, 1992.

——. *Lettres de Paul Gauguin à Emile Bernard*. Geneva: P. Cailler, 1954.

——. *Lettres de Paul Gauguin à son ami Daniel de Monfreid*. Toulouse: Imprimerie du Vignier, 1945.

Gogh, Vincent van. *The Complete Letters of Vincent van Gogh*. Boston: Little, Brown & Co., 1991.

———. *Correspondance générale*, Paris: Gallimard, Collection Biblos, 1990.

Pissarro, Camille. *Camille Pissarro: Letters to His Son Lucien*. Mamaroneck, N.Y.: Paul P. Appel, 1972.

THEO VAN GOGH

Collectie Theo van Gogh. Amsterdam: Stedelijk Museum, 1953.

Doiteau, Victor. "À quel mal succomba Theo van Gogh?"*Aesculape*, vol. 30, no. 1 (1940): 76–87.

Gachet, Paul. "Les médecins de Theo et Vincent van Gogh."*Aesculape* (March 1957): 4–37.

Gogh, Vincent Willem van. "Theo van Gogh without Vincent." *Art News*, vol. 52, no. 6 (October 1953): 24–30.

Hulsker, Jan. "1878: A Decisive Year in the Lives of Theo and Vincent." *Vincent: Bulletin of the Rijkmuseum Vincent van Gogh*, vol. 3, no. 3 (1974): 15–36.

———. "De Van Goghs en de Bongers." *Jong Holland*, no. 2 (1996).

———. *Vincent and Theo van Gogh: A Dual Biography*. Ann Arbor, Mich.: Fuller Publications, 1990.

———. "What Theo Really Thought of Vincent." *Vincent: Bulletin of the Rijkmuseum Vincent van Gogh*, vol. 3, no. 2 (1974): 2–28.

Jansen, Leo, and Jan Robert, eds. *Brief Happiness: The Correspondence of Theo van Gogh and Jo Bonger*. Amsterdam: Van Gogh Museum and Waanders Publishers, 1999.

Kraus, G. *Les liens entre Theo et Vincent van Gogh*. Amsterdam: Editions de la Fondation Kröller-Müller and J. M. Meulenhoff, 1954.

Ozanne, Marie-Angélique, and Frédérique de Jode. "Theo, le second van Gogh d'Auvers sur Oise." *Vivre en Val-d'Oise*, no. 54 (February–March 1999): 19–23.

Rewald, John. "Theo van Gogh, Goupil and the Impressonists." *Gazette des Beaux-Arts* (January 1973): 1–108.

Stolwijk, Chris, and Richard Thomson. *Theo van Gogh 1857–1891*. Zwolle and Amsterdam: Van Gogh Museum and Waanders Publishers, 1999.

Tralbaut, Marc Edo. "Van Gogh: un document inédit." *Connaissance des Arts*, no. 102 (August 1960): 10–16.

Veth, Jan. "Theo van Gogh." *De Amsterdammer*, (February 2, 1891): 3.

Voskuil, P. H. A. "Het medisch dossier van Theo van Gogh." *Nederlands Tijdschrift voor Geneeskunde*, no. 136 (1990).

VINCENT VAN GOGH

Artaud, Antonin. *Van Gogh le suicidé de la société*. Paris: Gallimard, 1947.

Aurier, Albert. "Les Isolés, Vincent van Gogh." (Paris) *Mercure de France* (January 1890).

Bernard, Emile. "L'enterrement de Vincent van Gogh." *Arts-Documents*, no. 29 (February 1953).

———. "Souvenirs sur Van Gogh." *L'amour de l'Art*, no. 12 (December 1924): 393–400.

Bonafoux, Pascal. *Van Gogh: le soleil en face*. Paris: Gallimard, 1991.

Bonnat, Jean-Louis. *Van Gogh: l'écriture de l'œuvre*. Paris: PUF, 1994.

Cabanne, Pierre. *Qui a tué Vincent van Gogh?* Paris: Quai Voltaire, 1992.

Cannat, Noël. *Entre révolte et médiation: les outsiders des nouveaux acteurs sociaux: V. Nijinski, V. van Gogh, T. E. Lawrence*. Paris and Montreal: Editions de l'Harmattan, 1998.

Carrié, Adeline. "Les souvenirs d'Adeline Ravoux sur le séjour de Vincent van Gogh à Auvers sur Oise." *Les cahiers de Van Gogh*, "no. 1 (1956).

Cassee, Elly. "In Love: Vincent van Gogh's First True Love." *Journal 1996.* (Amsterdam: Van Gogh Museum, 1997).

Crimpen, Han van. *Van Gogh in Brabant*. Zwolle: Waanders Publishers, 1987.

Du Quesne–van Gogh, Elisabeth. *Vincent van Gogh raconté par sa sœur*. Paris: Hazan, 1982.

Forrester, Viviane. *Van Gogh ou l'enterrement dans les blés*. Paris: Editions du Seuil, 1983.

Gachet, Paul. *Les soixante-dix jours de Vincent van Gogh à Auvers sur Oise*. Saint-Ouen l'Aumône: Editions du Valhermeil, 1994.

Garcin, Serge. *Van Gogh*. Paris: Gembloux, 1981.

Gogh, Vincent van. *The Complete Letters of Vincent van Gogh*. Boston: Little, Brown & Co., 1991.

Gogh, Vincent Willem van. *Letters of Vincent van Gogh, 1886–1890*. London: The Scolar Press, Ltd., 1977.

Jouffroy, Jean-Pierre. *La raison de Vincent van Gogh*. Paris: Messidor, 1990.

Laporte, Roger. *La loi de l'alternance*. Paris: Fourbis, 1997.

Leprohon, Pierre. *Vincent van Gogh*. Paris: Editions Corymbe, 1972.

Martin, Henri-André. *La maladie de van Gogh: le mystère d'une fin tragique*. Paris: Buchet-Chastel, 1994.

Mauron, Charles. *Van Gogh: études psychocritiques*. Paris: José Corti, 1976.

——. *Vincent et Theo van Gogh, une symbiose*. Amsterdam: Instistuut voor Modern Kunst, 1953.

Millon, Claude. *Vincent van Gogh et Auvers-sur-Oise*. Pontoise: Graphédis, 1998.

Miralles, Francesc. *Van Gogh*. Paris: Menges, 1994.

Monneret, Jean. *Vincent van Gogh au Salon des Indépendants 1888, 1889, 1890, 1891 ou la passion selon Vincent*. Paris: Société des Artistes Indépendants, 1990.

Monsel, Philippe. *Van Gogh 1853–1890*. Paris: Cercle d'Art, 1997.

Mothe, Alain. *Vincent van Gogh à Auvers-sur-Oise*. Paris: Editions du Valhermeil, 1987.

Perruchot, Henri. *La vie de van Gogh*. Paris: Marabout, 1981.

Pickvance, Ronald. *Van Gogh in Arles*. New York: The Metropolitan Museum of Art, 1984.

——. *Van Gogh in Saint-Rémy and Auvers*. New York: The Metropolitan Museum of Art, 1987.

Pickvance, Ronald, comp. *A Great Artist Is Dead: Letters of Condolence on Vincent van Gogh's Death*. Zwolle: Waanders Publishers, 1992.

Piérard, Louis. "Van Gogh au pays noir." *Mercure de France* (July 1913): 976–111.

Plazy, Gilles. *Les chemins de van Gogh.* Paris: Editions du Chêne, 1997.

Porot, Didier. *Van Gogh ou le Hollandais volant.* Rueil-Malmaison: Geigy, 1989.

Stiles Wylie, A. "Vincent's Childhood and Adolescence." *Bulletin of the Rijksmuseum Vincent van Gogh*, vol. 4, no. 2 (1975).

Stokvis, B. J. *Nasporingen omtrent Vincent van Gogh in Brabant.* Amsterdam: S. L. Van Looy, 1926.

Sweetman, David. *The Love of Many Things: A Life of Vincent van Gogh.* London: Hodder & Stoughton, 1990.

Tralbaut, Marc Edo. *Van Gogh, le mal aimé.* Lausanne: Edita, 1969.

Van Gogh à Paris. (exh. cat.) Paris: Publication du ministère de la Culture et de la Communication, 1988.

Varenne, Daniel. *Van Gogh: Zundert–Auvers.* Perigueux: Fanlac, 1989.

Welsh-Ovcharov, Bogomila. *Vincent van Gogh: His Paris Period 1886–1888.* Utrecht and The Hague: Editions Victorine, 1976.

Artistic Context

Ambrière, Madeleine. *Dictionnaire du XIXe siècle européen.* Paris: PUF, 1997.

Bernard, Emile. "Julien Tanguy." *Mercure de France* (December 1908): 600–616.

Bouin, Philippe, and Christian-Philippe Chanut. *Histoire française des foires et des expositions universelles.* Paris: Editions du Nesle, 1980.

Cachin, Françoise, ed. *L'art du XIXe siècle.* Paris: Editions Citadelles, 1990.

Distel, Anne. *Les collectionneurs des Impressionnistes: amateurs et marchands.* Paris: La Bibliothèque des Arts, 1989.

Donnay, Maurice. *Autour du Chat Noir.* Paris: Grasset, Les cahiers rouges, 1996.

Dubosc. *Soixante ans dans les ateliers d'artistes.* Paris: Calmann-Levy, 1900.

Gachet, Paul. *Deux amis des Impressionnistes: le docteur Gachet et Mürer,*

Paris: Editions des Musées nationaux, 1956.

Gauguin, Paul. *Avant et Après*. Paris: Editions de La Table Ronde, 1994.

Gauzi, François. *Lautrec, mon ami*. Paris: La Bibliothèque des Arts, 1992.

Goncourt, Edmond, and Jules de Goncourt. *Journal, Mémoires de la vie littéraire*. 3 vols. Paris: Robert Laffont, Collection Bouquins, 1989.

Joyant, Maurice. *Henri de Toulouse-Lautrec, 1864-1901*. 2 vols. Paris: H. Floury, 1926–27.

Lafont-Couturier, Hélène. "La maison Goupil ou la notion d'œuvre originale remise en question." *Revue de l'art*, no. 112 (second trimester 1996): 59–69.

Monneret, Sophie. *L'impressionnisme et son époque*. 2 vols. Paris: Robert Laffont, Collection Bouquins, 1987.

Ory, Pascal. *L'exposition universelle*. Paris: Ramsay, 1982.

Pingeot, Anne, ed. *Paris–Bruxelles, Bruxelles–Paris, les relations artistiques entre la France et la Belgique, 1848–1914*. (exh. cat.) Paris: Galeries nationales du Grand Palais: 1997.

Rewald, John. *Post-Impressionism: From Van Gogh to Gauguin*. New York: The Museum of Modern Art, 1956.

Roberts-Jones, Philippe. *Bruxelles, fin de siècle*. Paris: Flammarion, 1994.

Sillevis, John, Ronald de Leeuw, and Charles Dumas. *L'Ecole de La Haye, les maîtres hollandais du XIXe Siècle*. Paris: Grand Palais, 1983.

Vaisse, Pierre. *La troisième République et les peintres*. Paris: Flammarion, 1995.

Velter, André, ed. *Les poètes du Chat Noir*. Paris: Poésie, Gallimard, 1996.

Walter, Rodolphe. "L'Exposition Universelle de 1878." *L'Oeil*, no. 280 (November 1972): 38–45.

White, Harrison C., and Cynthia A. White. *Canvases and Careers: Institutional Change in the French Painting World*. New York: Wiley, 1965.

PHOTO CREDITS

Horse and Two Women, sketch in letter 398 from Vincent to Theo, Drenthe, October, 13, 1883. Van Gogh Museum (Vincent van Gogh Foundation), Amsterdam

PAGE 98: Vincent van Gogh, *Open Bible, Extinguished Candle, and a Novel,* 1885. Van Gogh Museum (Vincent van Gogh Foundation), Amsterdam

PAGE 112: Vincent van Gogh, *View from Vincent's room on the Rue Lepic,* 1887. Collection Vincent van Gogh Foundation/ Van Gogh Museum, Amsterdam

PAGE 133: Vincent van Gogh, *Gardens on Montmartre,* 1887. Stedelijk Museum, Amsterdam, The Netherlands. Copyright © Photo Marburg/Art Resource, NY

PAGE 138: Johanna Bonger. Photograph by J.D. van Rosmalen Jr. Van Gogh Museum (Vincent van Gogh Foundation), Amsterdam

PAGE 146: Vincent van Gogh, *Self-Portrait with Bandaged Ear,* 1889. The Samuel Courtauld Trust, Courtauld Institute of Art Gallery, London

PAGE 155: Theo van Gogh and Johanna Bonger's wedding announcement sent to Vincent van Gogh, 1889. Van Gogh Museum (Vincent van Gogh Foundation), Amsterdam

PAGE 175: Johanna van Gogh-Bonger and Vincent Willem van Gogh. Van Gogh Museum (Vincent van Gogh Foundation), Amsterdam

PAGE 178: Paul-Ferdinand Gachet, *Vincent van Gogh on his Deathbed,* 1890. Van Gogh Museum (Vincent van Gogh Foundation), Amsterdam

PAGE 210: Meijer de Haan, *Theo van Gogh,* 1889. Van Gogh Museum (Vincent van Gogh Foundation), Amsterdam

PAGE 215: Graves of Vincent and Theo van Gogh in Auvers-sur-Oise. Van Gogh Museum (Vincent van Gogh Foundation), Amsterdam

INDEX

49, 59–60; health, 30, 37, 56, 118, 148–52, 157–59, 171, 176–77, 182–83; lack of direction, 31–32; letters to Theo, 29–30, 37–38, 44, 49–50, 51–52, 62, 77, 88–90, 94–95; in London, 46, 52–53, 59–60; mouth surgery, 115; nephew and, 171, 177, 181–82, 198; opinion of art dealers, 101–2; paintings, 72, 91, *92, 94, 98*, 106, 107, 108, *112*, 114, *133*, 134, *146*, 162, 167, *169*, 170, 174, 189; in Paris, 109–11, 113–23, 185–88; personality, 28, 96, 120, 158–59; posthumous success, 199–203, 212–13; reaction to Jo's pregnancy, 164–65; reconciliation with Theo, 107–8; religion and, 56–58, 61, 71–77; at Saint-Remy, 157–58; as teacher, 60–61; temper, 53, 54, 91–92, 99–102; Theo and, 29–30, 36–37, 47, 75–78, 104, 123–24, 165–66, 214–15; women and, 47, 51–52, 87, 89–90, 109, 153
Gogh, Vincent van (stillborn), 22
Gogh, Vincent van (uncle), 19, *23*, 32, 39–40, 70, 105; death, 135; health, 39, 40, 62, 75; as nephews' mentor, 32–33, 38–40, 53, 56, 71–72
Gogh, Vincent W. van (son), 171, 173–74, *175*, 177, 198, 212–13
Gogh, Willemina van (sister), 22, *25*, 106, 107, 121–22, 124, 125, 135–36, 150–51, 153, 162, 189, 202–3, 206, 215
Goudeau, Emile, 86, 87
Goupil, Adolphe, 40, 127
Goupil & Cie, 32–33, 36, 39–40, *41*, 42–51, 67–68, 78–80, 93–95, 101–2. *See also* Boussod et Valadon
Groux, Henry de, 172
Guillaumin, Armand, 81, 85, 111, 118, 127, 129, 130, 186, 200, 203, 213
Guyotin (collector), 102

Haan, Meijer de, 125, 200, *210*, 213
Haanebeek, Annette, 47, 55–58
Haanebeek, Caroline, 47, 70
Hirschig, Anton, 194, 196
Houten, Joan van, 70, 105, 199

Isaäcson, Joseph J., 125, 160, 168

Japanese art, 67, 120, 123, 132

Jones, Slade, 60–61, 70
Joyant, Maurice, 206

Kahn, Gustave, 128
Kraus, G., 150–52, 185, 198
Kröller-Muller, Hélène, 212

Linden, Annie van der, 137, 144–45, 181–82, 187, 193, 197
Loyer, Eugenie, 52

Manet, Edouard, 67, 85, 127, 213
Maris, Jacobus, 49, 50
Matisse, Henri, 212
Mauron, Charles, 150
Maus, Octave, 166–67, 171, 202
Mauve, Anton, 49, 50, 134
Meissonier, Jean-L.-E., 68, 136
Mesdag, Hendrik, 50, 190
Michelet, Jules, 52, 56, 57
Millet, Jean, 43, 67, 91, 114, 213
Monet, Claude, 81, 85, 102, 108, 111, 120, 126–29, 136–37, 152, 161, 167, 176, 179, 189, 200, 206
Monticelli, Adolphe-J.-T., 123, 213
Moreau, Gustave, 111
Morisot, Berthe, 81, 111

Paris: art dealers, 80, 111; exhibitions, 110–11, 120, 130–33, 163, 166–67, 171–72, 174, 176, 186, 201, 202, 212; Montmartre, 75, 78–79, 84–87, 119, 193; ninth arrondissement, 79–80; World's Fair, 63, 65–72
Petit, Georges, 80, 111, 126–27, 131
Pissarro, Camille, 81, 85, 102, 108, 111, 119, 126, 127, 129–31, 136, 152, 160–61, 166–68, 174, 176, 180, 196, 200–201, 203–4, 209, 213
Pissarro, Lucien, 111, 127, 160–61, 166, 195, 196, 213
Portier, A., 108, 113
Prevost, Benoît Louis, 187
Proudhon, Pierre Joseph, 161

Raffaëlli, Jean, 85, 86, 180, 213
Ravoux (innkeeper), 196, 197
Renoir, Pierre-A., 81, 84, 85, 102, 111, 120, 126, 128, 136, 161, 172, 179
Rey, Félix, 148, 154, 157
Rodin, Auguste, 43, 68, 131